# BUILDING TEAMS
# FOR YOUR
# SMALL BUSINESS

by  Robert B. Maddux

## U.S. CHAMBER OF COMMERCE

SMALL
BUSINESS
INSTITUTE™

# CREDITS

Editor: Janis Paris

Layout/Design: ExecuStaff

Cover Design: Barry Littmann

Library of Congress 95-74820
ISBN-1-56052-365-4

# ABOUT THE USCC SMALL BUSINESS INSTITUTE

The U.S. Chamber of Commerce Small Business institute was formed to provide practical education and training resources for small business professionals and employees. The Institute offers practical and informative materials in:

- Marketing and Sales
- Budgeting and Finance
- Legal Issues
- Human Relations and Communication
- Productivity
- Quality and Customer Service
- Supervision, Management and Leadership

These ready reference materials, created for the U.S. Chamber by Crisp Publications, contain a wealth of useful advice for small businesses. The personal involvement exercises provide an opportunity to immediately apply what has been learned to your business.

While learning, it is easy to earn a  Small Business Institute Certificate of Completion and valuable Continuing Education Units (CEUs). For more information or to enroll, call 800-884-2880.

# THE U.S. CHAMBER OF COMMERCE
# SMALL BUSINESS INSTITUTE

► **High Quality**
Up-to-date and to-the-point training and educational materials are selected by small business professionals.

► **Practical and Easy to Use**
You can immediately put to use the proven tips and techniques.

► **Cost-effective**
The courses come to you—you don't have to spend money on travelling to a training site or pay costly tuition.

► **Design Your Own Program**
Choose those courses that interest you most and meet the specific needs of your company.

► **Self-paced**
Learn when your schedule permits. Complete the coursework on your time.

► **Recognition and Reward**
Business owners and employees can earn Continuing Education Units (CEUs) as well as a Small Business Institute Certificate of Completion to recognize the achievement.

► **Quality Guaranteed**
All materials are unconditionally guaranteed. If you are not totally satisfied, simply return course materials within 30 days for a complete refund. No questions asked.

# INTRODUCTION

People who undertake the start up, acquisition and/or operation of a small business are consumed by a mountain of legal requirements, contracts, budgets, marketing plans and an endless array of other details pertaining to operating the business. These of course include space acquisition, equipment, tools, hardware, raw materials and operating capital.

It is not hard under these circumstances to overlook the most important contributors to your future success—the people who will manage and/or do the work, present it to the customer and deliver the finished product. Frequently, the owner assumes the acquisition, care and nurturing of the human resource can wait until he/she can get around to it. Many businesses have gone straight down the tubes because of this attitude—everything else had been done but those who had to stand and deliver were not ready and the organization could not function.

This book is a guide based on extensive experience in both large and small business environments and is designed to cut to the core of the essentials in managing the human side of the enterprise. The sooner you read the book in its entirety the sooner you can begin to profit from the content. It is arranged in sections, however, so that the small business owner can use it as a ready reference when concerned with "how to do" a variety of management tasks well. Concepts are tied to business reality to give you "best practice" applications.

The first few chapters will walk you through concepts of management and team building. Management, as presented in this book, is seen as a *process* rather than a *role*. Thus it is interactive. Employees are approached as vital resources, individuals who give their best when they are considered to be valued members of a team.

The next few chapters concern hiring practices: assessing a vacancy, coming up with a detailed job description, planning an interview and customizing it to each candidate, documenting the selection process, respecting equal-opportunity legislation, following up on the interview, and making the evaluation. Team aspects are emphasized throughout. Of particular interest is the detailed information on questioning. This material teaches you to get and give information: It helps you create an atmosphere of open communication, get the most detailed answers you can, and provide enough information to your candidate so that they can make an informed decision.

Next, come the skills that you can help your team members enhance: communication, trust in the team and other team members, conflict resolution, and problem solving. In these sections, employees are encouraged to participate in both their own training and development as well as to help establish goals and standards for the entire company.

Almost everyone who has ever supervised someone else has been faced with the trade-off of needing to delegate tasks, but encountering difficulty in training someone to help. This book will first help you assess your own attitudes toward delegation, some of which might be holding you back, and teach you how to choose the tasks to delegate and the right people to do them.

Leadership is a vital aspect of a well-functioning team. The final chapter on coaching defines the role and responsibilities of necessary leadership. You can use this information to check and improve your own style and as a set of guidelines when working with employees functioning as team leaders.

# CONTENTS

# CONTENTS (continued)

# CONTENTS (continued)

# CHAPTER ONE

# MANAGEMENT AS A FOUR-STEP PROCESS

## OVERVIEW OF THE MANAGE-MENT PROCESS

Management is the *process of working through individuals and groups to accomplish organizational goals and objectives.*

When an owner starts or buys a business, there is an extremely important relationship that must be developed with employees and an important set of tasks that must be undertaken. These tasks are generally referred to as the management process. The owner's skill in managing this process will have a significant impact on the success of the business.

Management practitioners and scholars vary widely in their definitions of the management process. These differences are usually nothing more than a choice of words. Some group similar functions into broad categories—others prefer an extensive list of individual functions.

The management process for our purposes consists of four primary functions. These are: planning, organizing, motivating, and controlling.

This chapter will give you an opportunity to expand your understanding of these functions.

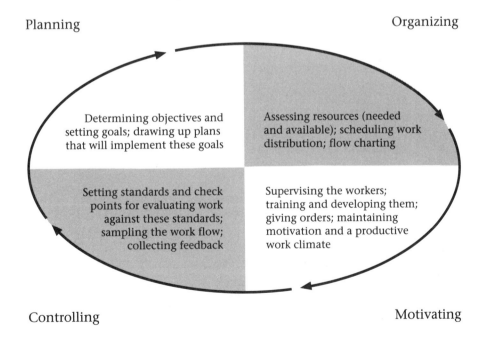

Planning

Organizing

Determining objectives and setting goals; drawing up plans that will implement these goals

Assessing resources (needed and available); scheduling work distribution; flow charting

Setting standards and check points for evaluating work against these standards; sampling the work flow; collecting feedback

Supervising the workers; training and developing them; giving orders; maintaining motivation and a productive work climate

Controlling

Motivating

# Planning

Planning is the thinking that precedes doing. It is concerned with setting goals and objectives for a business and with preparing plans and schedules to accomplish them. In the list below, the following are important elements in planning:

1. Gathering the thoughts and ideas of the employees who are directly involved, as well as your own thoughts and ideas.

2. Formulating and issuing policies and procedures to accomplish goals and objectives.

3. Examining alternatives and selecting the activities and programs that will lead to successful results.

4. Establishing timetables and completion targets in keeping with priorities.

5. Determining standards of performance and how results will be measured.

6. Identifying the resources necessary for task accomplishment—people, time, money, material—and determining their availability.

# Organizing

Once planning is underway, organizing becomes essential. Resources—people, capital, equipment, raw materials, facilities—must be brought together in the most productive way to accomplish goals and objectives. You must prepare to handle all these issues:

1. Appropriate staffing—the right number of people with the essential skills to perform the work that has to be done.

2. Delineation of responsibility and authority.

3. Alignment of major functions and structuring of the component parts into effective work units and teams.

4. Manuals, administrative guides, and other tools to make known how responsibility has been assigned and authority delegated.

5. A communications system for reporting and coordination between people and organizations.

6. Methods of problem solving and conflict resolution.

7. Facilities and equipment needed for task accomplishment.

## Motivating

Motivation, along with planning and organizing, plays an important part in the level of performance that will be achieved in any endeavor. Check your views. Review the following statements on motivation. Are any of them a surprise to you?

1. The needs and desires of employees have a great deal of bearing on motivation.

2. It is important to create an environment in which employees can meet their needs while meeting the needs of the organization.

3. Results generally improve when people are able to participate in deciding what the results should be.

4. Motivation to achieve results is improved when employees are recognized for their contributions.

5. Studies have shown that communication has much to do with motivation.

6. Coaching and training tend to raise personal levels of motivation.

7. Motivation to achieve results usually increases as employees are given authority to make decisions affecting those results.

8. Good supervisors pay close attention to the way employees respond when they assign work.

## Controlling

Controlling is concerned with results. It involves follow-up to compare results with plans and to make adjustments when results differ from expectations. Controlling does *not* require punishing employees who have missed their targets or limiting employee authority to minor details. Controlling requires:

1. Devising ways to assess whether goals, objectives, or standards have been met in a timely and cost-effective manner.

2. Formulating methods by which the use of the various resources can be measured and evaluated for future planning purposes.

3. Establishing systems that provide feedback at key points as the work progresses, so that deviations from plan can be identified, evaluated, and acted upon.

4. Reporting the status of activities and projects to those who need to know.

# BECOMING AN EFFECTIVE PLANNER

Planning is the thinking that precedes the work. If planning is not done, time and effort is usually wasted.

Teams need to know why they exist, what they are supposed to accomplish and who else is involved. If these areas are fuzzy, frustration is the result. Team members expect their leader to know the direction they are to take, and how they are to coordinate with other groups to reach their goals. To accomplish this, effective planning is required. Effective planning includes the following elements:

1. Projecting what will be needed to keep the business profitable in the future.

2. Articulating organizational needs (including those of the team) into team goals and objectives.

3. Formulating implementation plans by examining alternatives and selecting activities which lead to successful results.

4. Identifying resources needed to achieve goals (people, time, money, materials and facilities) and insuring they are available.

5. Establishing time lines and completion target dates.

6. Determining standards of performance and how results will be measured.

Employees can make important contributions to planning once they become committed in the process. If you coordinate planning well, your team leadership will be much more effective. If you need to improve—do it now!

# STRENGTHENING YOUR ORGANIZING SKILLS

Once planning is underway, organization becomes important. Resources—people, capital, raw materials, and technology—must be coordinated effectively to achieve team goals. Team members look to the leader for direction and the allocation of resources. If organization is poor, the group will become confused, discouraged, argumentative, uncooperative, and defensive. Teamwork will be impossible.

Leaders must be well organized and capable of helping the team organize itself to accomplish established goals. One of the strengths of a good leader is the ability to see a future for the organization that is better in some important ways than what currently exists.

This view must then be communicated in such a way employees can organize their resources to achieve the desired results.

Some key aspects of organization are listed below:

1. Dividing work into logical tasks and groupings.

2. Knowing how to secure the resources required to achieve goals.

3. Being comfortable assigning tasks, resources, and responsibility to team members on the basis of functions and skills.

4. Establishing guidelines in order to coordinate activities between team members and other groups involved with the outcome.

5. Making it a practice to design information systems which assure appropriate feedback as the work progresses.

6. Establishing communications networks to insure there is a free flow of information up, down, and across organizational lines.

Employees can make important contributions to the organizing process because of their knowledge and experience. Employee involvement can enhance teamwork and efficiency. The better your organizational skills, the stronger you should be as a leader. If you need to improve—do it now!

# BUILDING A CLIMATE FOR MOTIVATION

People work for a variety of reasons. What is important for one person might have little significance to another. Motivation is personal and owners must get to know individual employees in order to learn what motivates them. Some people work for basic survival needs, while others are seeking security. Some work to fulfill ego satisfaction or something even deeper.

Establishing yourself as a strong leader requires an understanding of people and what motivates them. Those who understand can create a climate in which team members can meet individual needs while achieving team goals.

An owner must be sensitive to employee needs and design ways to meet them while achieving the goals of the organization. No single technique works for everyone.

Your team members need your leadership to help them understand the issues and to focus their effort in the right places. When you have your act together, you can help your employees do the same. Your efforts, and theirs, will create a work climate that is meaningful and mutually supportive. Here are some tips to make it happen successfully.

▶ Reflect a positive, "can and will do" attitude.

▶ Demonstrate personal flexibility.

▶ Communicate your vision of the future and how it is bridged to the present.

▶ Identify and talk through the concerns of each team member.

▶ Discuss and clarify organizational, personal and employee objectives. Eliminate ambiguities.

▶ Help team members assess their current role, express your expectations and together develop a plan to meet team objectives.

▶ Determine what employees consider to be problems and involve them in finding solutions.

▶ Fix quickly things that are broken.

▶ Show team members the importance of letting go of the past, focusing on the present and anticipating change in the future.

▶ Help employees determine how their personal career goals can be achieved or made more realistic.

▶ Encourage employees to show some initiative and to risk a little. They will grow in the process.

▶ Use delegation to educate and develop people.

▶ Devote whatever resources you have available to recognize and reward desired performance.

- ► Recognize genuine attempts to achieve as well as the achievements themselves.

- ► Make sure policies and procedures always support the accomplishment of objectives.

- ► Ask your employees frequently what might be happening that makes them uncomfortable and inhibits their performance.

- ► Be sure your behavior and communication practices continue to be consistent and congruent with what you expect from others.

- ► If your organization is in transition, discuss the emotional impacts with employees so they will understand what they are experiencing is normal. Do help them move on to a new commitment as soon as possible.

# ESTABLISHING A CONTROL SYSTEM

Once a project has begun, a control system is needed to make sure it will progress according to plan, and the ultimate objective will be achieved. In other words, as the action progresses, modifying and adjusting this plan may be necessary to keep the team focused and on target. This process is called controlling. Controls should be established during the planning process and be as simple as possible.

Once a control system is in place, the leader and the team can compare what is happening with what was expected. Based on the ongoing results, it may be necessary to revise the objective, modify the plan, reorganize, or take some added motivational steps or other appropriate action. Some important aspects of controlling are listed below:

1. Establishing control elements as part of the project plan.

2. Setting up time schedules and check points to measure progress.

3. Encouraging feedback from team members throughout the project.

4. Evaluating problems or deviations from plans, and then constructing a new action plan which is timely and appropriate.

5. Adjusting objectives, plans, resources, or motivational factors as required to meet the organizational goals.

6. Communicating progress and plan changes to those who need to know.

In a team situation, employees should, by virtue of their involvement, do much of the controlling. If you need to improve your skills in this area—do it now!

**Your Turn**

*Answer the following:*

▶ What are the most important things you need to learn about planning, organizing, controlling, and motivating?

▶ Where and when can you learn what you need to know?

▶ Who is responsible for checking results against goal achievement?

▶ What happens when goals are not met?

# CASE STUDY

## Which Supervisor Would You Prefer?

This case study will give you a chance to apply what you have learned.

Morgana and Jeff have just been promoted to their first supervisory position. Both have had considerable experience as Senior Micro-Technicians prior to the promotion. Morgana and Jeff shared plans for making the transition from technician to supervisor one day during lunch.

Morgana volunteered that she plans to concentrate on defining the work that needs to be done, and then provide her employees with precise goals and standards. Because of her experience and knowledge, she will also prepare a detailed performance plan for each employee. She feels this approach will ensure the goals are met while giving her the control she needs to get the job done.

Jeff responded by saying he had already secured the owner's agreement to take a supervisory skills course to insure he understood the management process. In the meantime, however, Jeff indicated he plans to involve his group in day-to-day planning, organizing and problem solving. Jeff is confident of his ability but feels every member of his staff is competent and can make important contributions to the group's effectiveness. He also feels that individuals need the satisfaction that comes from being involved in a project.

Which of these supervisors would you rather have working for you?

_____

_____

_____

Compare your response with the author's.

# Response to Case Study

It is good that both Morgana and Jeff recognize the importance of clear goals and plans. Employees who have limited knowledge or expertise may appreciate Morgana's approach because they have a great deal to learn. As they learn under Morgana's management, however, they may feel too restricted to share their ideas. New methods, better products, and simpler ways to achieve objectives might not be forthcoming. Experienced employees may feel that way at the outset.

Experienced employees will appreciate Jeff's approach because it provides a needed outlet to contribute. They will feel free to improve the effectiveness of the group while improving their own. Employees with lesser skills will be encouraged to learn so they too can become more productive and contribute. Jeff's employees will appreciate his decision to participate in supervisory training because they appreciate a manager who knows the basics.

# ASK YOURSELF

With how many of the following statements can you agree?

► I am confident about the future of my business.

► My skills in planning, organizing, motivating, and controlling are well above average.

► I have a successful planning process in place.

► I follow up to be sure goals are accomplished.

# CHAPTER TWO

# TEAM-BUILDING CONCEPTS

# GROUPS: FUNDA-MENTAL UNITS OF ORGANIZA-TIONS

From the beginning of time people have formed *groups*. Groups provide the basis for family living, protection, waging war, government, recreation, and work. Group behavior has ranged from total chaos to dramatic success, but it is increasingly evident that groups enjoy their greatest success when they become more productive units called *teams*.

## Limitations of Groups

Managers in many organizations seem content with group performance. This is often because they hold to a traditional concept of leadership—that of the hierarchy, with one person on top controlling and perhaps limiting the input of group members. These managers have not thought beyond *what is being accomplished* to *what might be achieved* under slightly different circumstances.

Other leaders using the same number of people, doing similar tasks with the same technology, somehow manage to improve productivity dramatically by establishing a climate where people are willing to give their best and work together in teams.

## Increased Productivity Is the By-Product of Teamwork

When productive teams are compared with less productive groups, there are some important differences involving the application of team concepts. Here is an example:

A study was made of twenty coal mines operating in the same geologic structure, drawing from the same labor pool, and subject to the same governmental regulations. Productivity was measured in tons of coal produced per employee per shift.

The mine with the highest productivity delivered 242 tons per employee contrasted with the lowest which mined 58 tons per employee. The other mines were somewhere in between.

Conclusions from this study were summarized as follows: "The primary difference was the way in which company management worked with the employees. The most productive mine provided employees with significantly more individual responsibility and involvement in goal setting and problem solving."

# HOW GROUPS ARE LIMITED

Traditional groups have certain qualities in common that tend to limit the creative input of all but the most assertive members.

For instance, members think they are grouped together for administrative purposes only. Thus individuals work independently—sometimes at cross purposes with others. They tend to focus on themselves because they are not sufficiently involved in planning the unit's objectives. They approach their job simply as a hired hand. In this environment, members are told what to do rather than being asked what the best approach would be. Suggestions are not encouraged.

Members of traditional work groups distrust the motives of colleagues because they do not understand the role of other members. Expressions of opinion or disagreement are considered divisive or nonsupportive. Members are sometimes so cautious about what they say that real understanding is not possible. Game playing may occur and communications traps set to catch the unwary.

Skills may be wasted. Members may receive good training but are limited in applying it to the job by the supervisor or other group members.

And finally, conflicts can get out of control. Members find themselves in conflict situations which they do not know how to resolve. Their supervisor may put off intervention until serious damage is done.

In short, members may or may not participate in decisions affecting the team. Conformity often appears more important than positive results.

# GROUP-CENTERED MANAGERS

Group-centered owner/managers may not realize that there is a more creative way to get the best from their team members—especially if they have been reasonably successful in the past.

Let's begin by identifying behaviors of the group-centered manager. Identify those that fit you. The next sections will describe more productive approaches you might like to try out.

Group-centered managers often have an overriding concern to meet current goals. This can inhibit thought about what might be accomplished through enhancing member contributions.

They are often reactive to others, finding it easier to go along with the crowd. They are willing to involve people in planning and problem solving to some extent—but within limits.

Ask yourself if you have ever resented or distrusted employees who knew their jobs better than you. As a manager, do you ever control information and communicate only what group members need to know?

Do you see group problem solving as a waste of time, or an abdication of managerial responsibility? Or have you ever ignored conflict between staff members or with other groups?

Are you sometimes slow to recognize individual or group achievements?

Finally, do you sometimes modify group agreements to suit personal convenience?

# TEAM BUILDING: A NEW STYLE OF MANAGEMENT

Team leaders exhibit different styles from those who are content managing a group. These leaders encourage and profit from the contributions of the highly valued individuals committed to their team.

In this environment, members recognize their interdependence and understand both personal and team goals are best accomplished with mutual support. Time is not wasted struggling over "turf" or attempting personal gain at the expense of others. They feel a sense of ownership for their jobs and unit because they are committed to goals they helped establish.

In a team environment, members contribute to the organization's success by applying their unique talent and knowledge to team objectives. They are encouraged to develop further skills and apply what they learn on the job. They receive the support of the team.

The atmosphere is a climate of trust and members are encouraged to openly express ideas, opinions, disagreements and feelings. Questions are welcomed. Members make an effort to understand each other's point of view.

Team members recognize that conflict is a normal aspect of human interaction but they view such situations as an opportunity for new ideas and creativity. They work to resolve conflict quickly and constructively.

Members participate in decisions affecting the team but understand their leader must make a final ruling whenever the team cannot decide, or an emergency exists. Positive results, not conformity are the goal.

# HOW TEAM LEADERS FUNCTION

Given today's rapid rate of organizational change, and the changing needs of people, it is important for those "in charge" to re-evaluate and modify their styles on a regular basis. This is the only way they can make the adaptations necessary to continue to be effective.

In this section, we will identify how team-centered leadership differs from group-centered management. Plan to make any needed changes in your style and evaluate the results carefully. Keep making adjustments until you achieve the results desired. Stay on the alert for additional ways to improve your leadership.

A team-centered manager does not forget current goals but he or she can be a visionary about what the people can achieve as a team. A team leader shares this vision with others. If you want to be a team leader, strive to exhibit personal style and stimulate excitement and action. Inspire teamwork and mutual support.

Can you get people involved and committed? Make it easy for others to see opportunities for teamwork. Allow people to perform. Look for people who want to excel and can work constructively with others. Remember, your role is to encourage and facilitate this behavior.

A team leader considers problem solving the responsibility of team members. Set an example by communicating fully and openly. Welcome questions. Allow the team to do its own filtering. Mediate conflict before it becomes destructive.

Make an effort to see that both individual and team accomplishments are recognized at the right time in an appropriate manner. Remember that if you are honest and keep commitments, you can expect the same in return.

# APPLYING TEAM CONCEPTS

A diverse group formed each year to compete in a sport is an excellent example of team building. Groups develop into "teams" when their common purpose is understood by all of the members. Within effective teams each member plays an assigned role using his or her talent to the best advantage. When the members integrate their skills to accentuate strengths and minimize weaknesses, team objectives are usually achieved. When on the other hand groups play as individuals, they usually fail. Most wins or losses are the result of "teamwork." In sports, feedback is often immediate. If teamwork is lacking, good managers can identify where the problems are and initiate corrective action in order to change things until the desired results are achieved.

On a sports team, a skilled manager has responsibility to help select the players, coordinate the team's effort, and oversee the playing of the game. However, all players must know their jobs, have the skill to do them well, and be committed to making a contribution to the team. Players and the manager communicate with one another, trust and support one another, and resolve their differences in a constructive manner. There is also a built-in reward system that meets both the needs of the team and the personal needs of individual players.

## Setting the Process in Motion

Like their athletic counterparts, groups organized to perform business, community, and governmental functions can achieve far more when they work as "teams." Unfortunately, many leaders fail to recognize and apply the same principles as they would coaching a sport. In a work organization they do not understand how to transform their group into a productive team. One reason may be that feedback in the form of results is not as quick or dramatic as in athletics. Problems can go unnoticed and corrective action, if taken at all, can be slow in coming.

Effective teamwork knows no level. It is just as important among top executives as it is among middle managers, first line supervisors, or the rank and file. The absence of teamwork at any level (or between levels) will limit organizational effectiveness and can eventually kill an organization.

## Improve Your Team-Building Skills

You can be a successful leader and team builder or be a miserable failure. Note the factors that make the difference on page 23.

| Successful Leaders | Miserable Failures |
|---|---|
| Leaders who engage in mutual goal setting and open communication. | Those who establish arbitrary unilateral goals or standards. They may or may not communicate them to employees. |
| Leaders who establish clear, measurable expectations and provide a climate conducive to success. | Those who have not thought through what they expect or don't know how to measure success, thereby creating a threatening atmosphere in which to work. |
| Leaders who ask questions, listen carefully and appreciate and use the ideas of others. | Those who never seek the ideas of others or listen, yet have a solution for everyone else's problems. |
| Leaders who publicly recognize positive performance and privately correct improper performance when it occurs. | Those who spend too much time looking for things that are wrong and too little looking for things that are right. |
| Leaders who give honest feedback on performance against mutually understood goals. | Those who accept substandard performance or misrepresent it in providing feedback. |
| Leaders who follow through on their commitments. | Those who do not take their commitments seriously. |

## Getting Started

Your attitude will make a big difference in team building. When the concept of team building is understood and applied at all levels in an organization (or among colleagues in your profession) it becomes much easier to transform groups into teams throughout the organization. However, it is to any leader's advantage to develop a team whether others are doing so or not. A positive attitude toward team building is essential.

If you are waiting for a team to form automatically, it is going to be a long wait and in the meantime you will be limiting the success of your business and yourself. A thinking, proactive owner/manager will set the process in motion by immediately making a concerted effort to develop solid management skills.

---

*Your Turn*  *Answer these questions:*

► List three benefits you could logically expect from applying team building concepts in your company.

► Identify possible barriers to team building and describe how you will overcome them.

► Which of your partners or employees is most likely to support team building and how can you enlist their aid?

---

# WHAT CAN TEAM BUILDING DO FOR ME?

It requires effort to establish and maintain teamwork. If a leader does not place a high value on teamwork, it will not occur. Teamwork takes conscious effort to develop and continuous effort to maintain, but the rewards can be great.

Leaders sometimes assign a low priority to team building because they have not considered the advantages that can accrue from a well executed team effort. Following are some results of team performance. Make a note of those you would like to achieve.

► Realistic, achievable goals can be established for the team and individual members because those responsible for doing the work contribute to their construction.

► Employees and leaders commit to support each other to make the team successful.

► Team members understand one another's priorities and help or support when difficulties arise.

► Communication is open. The expression of new ideas, improved work methods, articulation of problems and concerns is encouraged.

► Problem solving is more effective because the expertise of the team is available.

► Performance feedback is more meaningful because team members understand what is expected and can monitor their performance against expectations.

► Conflict is understood as normal and viewed as an opportunity to solve problems. Through open discussion it can be resolved before it becomes destructive.

► Balance is maintained between group productivity and the satisfaction of personal team members' needs.

► The team is recognized for outstanding results, as are individuals, for their personal contributions.

► Members are encouraged to test their abilities and try out ideas. This becomes infectious and stimulates individuals to become stronger performers.

► Team members recognize the importance of disciplined work habits and conform their behavior to meet team standards.

► Learning to work effectively as a team in one unit is good preparation for working as a team with other units. It also supports personal growth.

# ATTITUDES OF AN EFFECTIVE TEAM BUILDER

The following attitudes support team building. This scale will help identify your strengths, and determine areas where improvement would be beneficial. Circle the number that best reflects where you fall on the scale. The higher the number, the more the characteristic describes you. When you have finished, total the numbers circled in the space provided.

1. When I select employees I choose those who can meet the job requirements and work well with others.　　7 6 5 4 3 2 1

2. I give employees a sense of ownership by involving them in goal setting, problem solving, and productivity improvement activities.　　7 6 5 4 3 2 1

3. I try to provide team spirit by encouraging people to work together and to support one another on activities that are related.　　7 6 5 4 3 2 1

4. I talk with people openly and honestly and encourage the same kind of communication in return.　　7 6 5 4 3 2 1

5. I keep agreements with my people because their trust is essential to my leadership.　　7 6 5 4 3 2 1

6. I help team members get to know each other so they can learn to trust, respect, and appreciate individual talent and ability.　　7 6 5 4 3 2 1

7. I insure employees have the required training to do their job and know how it is to be applied.　　7 6 5 4 3 2 1

8. I understand that conflict within groups is normal, but work to resolve it quickly and fairly before it can become destructive.　　7 6 5 4 3 2 1

9. I believe people will perform as a team when they know what is expected, and what benefits will accrue.      7 6 5 4 3 2 1

10. I am willing to replace members who cannot or will not meet reasonable standards after appropriate coaching.      7 6 5 4 3 2 1

TOTAL _____

A score between 60 and 70 indicates a positive attitude toward people and the type of attitude needed to build and maintain a strong team. A score between 40 and 59 is acceptable and with reasonable effort team building should be possible for you. If you scored below 40, you need to carefully examine your attitude in light of current management philosophy.

# CASE STUDY

## Can This Owner Be Saved?

Case studies help provide insights you may not already possess. This case study will help you understand the importance of learning and applying team building concepts.

Mary Lou started her new business about three months ago. She has five employees. She has never supervised others before and has had little management training.

Although each employee has a different job with its own standards, the tasks are interrelated and the success of the business depends upon a cooperative effort. Mary Lou has worked hard to assign tasks, set deadlines, and solve problems in order to achieve the desired results. The poor skills of two employees, and the constant bickering within the group, however, has caused delays and personal frustration for everyone. Mary Lou would like to spend more time with her employees but paperwork seems to consume most of her time. Recently she also has begun to stay in her office more because of the hostility between the employees. Group productivity has fallen below target, and Mary Lou is increasingly afraid she may have to close her business.

What might Mary Lou do to save her business and turn performance around?

_____

_____

_____

_____

_____

_____

_____

## Response to Case Study

Mary Lou is in serious trouble. It will take real effort to turn things around. It appears Mary Lou is trapped by her office and her paperwork. She needs training to develop better competence and more confidence as a supervisor. Until Mary Lou learns to manage herself, she will be unable to manage anyone else. Her employees also seem untrained, unsure of themselves, and poorly disciplined. Until they understand their jobs better and recognize the importance of cooperating with each other, chaos will be the result.

Since Mary Lou's group is interdependent, it must work as a team to be successful. Mary Lou must try her best to learn and apply team concepts. Specifically, she must become a better leader and supervisor, build the skills and confidence of her employees, establish a better working climate, and institute an appropriate reward system. How to accomplish this is the basis for this book.

# ASK YOURSELF

► Do employees in your company, including supervisors and managers, function as groups or teams?

► What steps do you need to take initially to begin the team building process?

► Are there any compelling reasons to delay development of the team building process and beginning to reap the benefits?

► What steps do you need to take personally to make it happen?

# CHAPTER THREE

# ADDING TO YOUR TEAM: ASSESSING THE POSITION

## THE FIRST STEP

What is the first thing you should do when you have a vacant position? The best first step is to determine whether the vacancy needs to be filled. If the answer is "yes," the next question should be, "what qualifications are required for a replacement?" The answer requires a review of the job itself.

In addition to mere job duties, when assessing a position, be sure to include all the aspects that might influence a choice of candidates:

- ▶ Benefits

- ▶ Extra duties

- ▶ Advancement potential

- ▶ Description of your product or service

- ▶ Physical environment of the workplace

- ▶ Your organizational structure

- ▶ The temperaments of other colleagues on the team

*Your Turn*

*Answer the following:*

- ▶ What is your turnover rate?

- ▶ How many positions have you eliminated or added in the past year? Why?

- ▶ What rationale do you use to justify a new position?

## DETERMINING JOB REQUIREMENTS

A fundamental step in finding the best candidate is to determine the job requirements of the position to be filled. Supervisors often believe they know all aspects of each position and evaluate applicants accordingly. Often they simply look for someone *like the person being replaced.* They do not consider what might be achieved by a person with different qualifications who might better fit the actual job requirements. A thorough review of job requirements helps refresh and remind a supervisor of ways in which the job may have changed. If it has changed enough, it may be better performed by a person with different qualifications.

If a formal position description is not available, one should be prepared. Information about the job will fall into the following five categories:

1. **The Purpose of the Job:**

   - What is the ultimate product or service desired?
   - What is the relationship of this job to others in the organization?
   - What are the consequences of poor or missed performance?

2. **What the Job Holder Actually Does:**

   - What are the most important duties performed?
   - What are the secondary duties?
   - How often are the duties performed?
   - What is the nature and scope of decision making?

3. **How the Person Performs the Job:**

   - What are the reporting relationships?
   - What internal and external contacts are involved?
   - What are the general working conditions (place, hours, hazards, advantages, co-workers)?

4. **What Human Relations and Personal Skills Are Required:**

   - What interpersonal skills are required to support relationships with others?
   - Is the position detail oriented?
   - Is logic or reasoning required?

- What specific skills are absolutely essential?
- Is good grooming required?
- How important is attitude?

5. **What Physical Attributes Are Necessary:**

- Is physical strength required?
- Is size a factor?

  Note that judgments based on physical characteristics must be bona fide. If you elect not to hire a disabled person, you may be required to show:

  —Specifically how the disability prevents the person from doing the work.

  —How the person would create a health or safety hazard for others.

# ESTABLISHING QUALIFICATIONS

Minimum hiring qualifications for a position should be drawn directly from the job requirements. If it is an entry-level position, the potential of an individual to progress should be considered, but unreasonable qualifications should not be demanded for a new hire. For example, a college degree for an entry-level secretarial position is unrealistic. The possibility of an individual progressing to an assignment where a degree would be helpful does not justify this requirement at entry level.

Once key elements of the position have been established, critical performance factors should be identified.

For instance, a position classified "material coordinator" might be approached in the following way.

**Knowledge.** Knowledge requirements can be determined by examining the job structure, the type of materials coordinated, and the personal equipment involved.

**Clerical Skills.**   If records must be maintained on procedures or incoming and outgoing materials, they can be reviewed to determine the clerical skills required and the amount of detail involved.

**Interpersonal Skills.**   An examination of the type and scope of person-to-person transactions (and the conditions under which they occur) will determine the interpersonal skills requirements of the position and the need to function as a team player.

**Physical Characteristics.**   Observing the actual worksite and performance of the work being done will determine the physical attributes the work demands.

## Job Specification Worksheet

Preparing a job specification worksheet similar to this one prior to the actual interview is a good way to establish required qualifications.

1. List the most critical responsibilities of the job (make or break factors).

   **Example:**  **Administrative Assistant/Community Health Education**

   Word processing
   Filing
   Mail processing and distribution
   Completing administrative reports
   Answering telephones and receiving visitors

2. List the duties critical to the performance of each major responsibility.

   **Example:**  Word Processing

   Prepare general correspondence
   Prepare monthly activity reports
   Prepare copy for brochures
   Prepare statistical tables

3. List the critical skills and knowledge necessary to perform each duty.

   **Example:** Prepare copy for brochures—do page layout

   Prepare statistical summaries—understand basic math
   Draft general correspondence—be able to write clearly

4. List degree of skill required and whether it is mandatory, desired or will be taught.

   **Example:** Typing—55 wpm straight copy—mandatory
   Typing—30 wpm unarranged rough draft—desirable
   Spelling and grammar—error free—mandatory
   Basic math skills—mandatory
   Page layout—will train

5. List expected results.

   **Example:** Prepare attractive error-free documents that communicate clearly and concisely.

6. List the physical attributes necessary to perform the job.

   **Example:** Normal stooping and bending.
   Read fine print.
   Hear well enough to handle telephones.

7. List the behavioral attributes necessary to perform the job.

   **Example:** Daily communication with large numbers of diverse personalities. Must be cheerful and communicative.

# CASE STUDY

## Mary Ann's Replacement Problem

Mary Ann has operated her own computer services business for two years. During that time there have been many changes in hardware and software services.

Yesterday, one of Mary Ann's senior service representatives announced his decision to retire at the end of the month. Mary Ann is anxious to begin the search for a replacement but is not sure where to start. She has come up with the following checklist for herself.

▶ Review (and update if necessary) the job description for the position in question.

▶ Review staffing versus workload for the entire unit to determine if the position is still needed.

▶ Ask other departments serviced if their needs are being fully met by the skills and knowledge of the existing staff.

▶ Examine the possibility of reassigning existing staff members for either cross training or promotion.

▶ Review the knowledge and skills currently required in the position and weigh them against any changes in function that are planned for the future.

▶ Discuss job knowledge and skill requirements with the incumbent. What are considered to be the most critical?

## Response to Case Study

Before Mary Ann begins the search for candidates, she will want to complete the other steps. A vacancy offers the opportunity to take actions that could be difficult when fully staffed. A study of the position itself, the needs of the unit now and in the future, and the needs of those serviced, may lead to a variety of conclusions. These could include: elimination of the position, realignment of duties and functions within the unit to provide better service, a change in knowledge and skill requirements for the position, or a decision to cross train existing staff.

If there are functional changes ahead for the unit, this may be the ideal time to begin acquiring the new skills and knowledge that will be required. If Mary Ann concludes the incumbent should be replaced by a person of similar qualifications, she can begin the selection process with confidence she understands the position requirements and has fully considered her options.

# SUPPLYING THE APPLICANT WITH INFORMATION

Part of the interviewer's job is sharing information about the position and the organization with the applicant. It's a two-way street. You are evaluating the applicant and the applicant is evaluating you and the organization as a potential employer. After all, how can an applicant make a sound decision without all the facts?

You will want to present important job details and the organization's best points. In addition, you should have a basic information packet to give every candidate at the conclusion of the interview. Make sure the material is professional and polished. You will most likely reserve your strongest sales presentation for the most qualified candidates, but every applicant should leave the interview feeling well informed.

Be prepared to respond to a variety of questions. The persons most interested in the job will most likely include those who ask the toughest questions. They probably care the most and have done the most research.

## Describe the Job Itself

Describe the key duties and responsibilities to the extent the candidate has a clear picture of what the job entails. Review the tasks a new hire will be expected to perform immediately as well as those to be done as quickly as they can be assimilated. Describe the kind of training and support that will be provided.

### Discuss the Supervisor

To whom will the new employee report? What is that person's management style? How long has she/he been in the position? What are his/her outstanding strengths?

### Describe the Work Setting

Where will the work be done? Will the new employee have a private office? What type of technology is in use? Will other employees be supervised?

### State a Salary Range

While it is unnecessary to discuss a specific salary level during the early stages of the interview process, it is only fair to indicate the salary range being considered. If the rate for the position is fixed, tell the candidate the rate and why it is fixed. Benefits can be summarized during the early stages of screening and described in full if and when an offer is made.

### Give a Department Overview

What is its purpose and function? How many employees work there? How does it relate to the balance of the organization?

### Discuss the Company's Products and Operations

Understanding the nature of the business will help the applicant evaluate her/his interest in becoming a part of the organization. You cannot assume the candidate is familiar with what is manufactured or the services provided. What differentiates the products or services from those of the competition? Is the company privately or publicly held? How is the organization structured? What are its current primary goals? For the future?

### Present Appropriate Facts and Figures

How profitable is the company? How large is the plant? How many people does the organization employ? Is expansion or relocation planned?

# ASK YOURSELF

▶ Do you have written job descriptions for each job/position at your organization?

▶ Have you identified critical performance factors for each job/position?

▶ At the close of the interview, do you let the candidate know how and when the hiring decision will be made?

CHAPTER
FOUR

# THE
# ART
# OF
# INTERVIEWING

# INTERVIEW STYLES

Every interviewer brings a different personality to the interview depending on background and experience. This individual style, however, must be blended into an effective interviewing format if the outcome is to be successful. Several styles are described here, and you probably have a tendency to fall into one more than the others. Read each for its advantages and disadvantages to see what you might like to change in your own style.

## The "Eyeball" Interview

In this style, interviewers assume they can predict job performance on the basis of appearance, handshake and other cursory observations. It is very superficial and totally unreliable.

## The Friendly Chat

It can be a pleasant experience talking about sports, the weather, mutual experiences, etc. Unless controlled, however, the business purpose of the interview will never be achieved.

## The Inquisition

Some interviewers enjoy placing an applicant under stress to see how they react. The usual result is withdrawal by the candidate. Accordingly, little is learned about ability or performance.

## The Straight-Down-the-Middle Interview

The interviewer will ask a predetermined series of questions in a standard order. This interview is so stiff and inflexible that it does not permit the interviewer to explore areas of potential mutual interest. It also limits the candidate's expression of qualifications and personality.

## The Businesslike Interview

This interview is a social situation with a business purpose in which worthwhile information is exchanged between the parties. It does not begin until the interviewer has a clear understanding of the responsibilities of the job to be filled and an idea of the kind of person required to fulfill them.

This style is endorsed in this book.

# INTERVIEWER'S SELF-ASSESSMENT

Before we look at the selection interview process in detail, you might find it worthwhile to assess your interviewing skills.

This scale will help identify your strengths and determine areas to improve. Circle the number that best reflects where you fall on the scale. The higher the number, the more like the characteristic you feel you are. When you have finished, total the numbers circled.

1. I analyze job requirements thoroughly before beginning the selection process.  
   5 4 3 2 1

2. I study qualifications of applicants in light of the job requirements *before* each interview.  
   5 4 3 2 1

3. I develop a unique interview plan based on item 2.  
   5 4 3 2 1

4. I begin each interview by establishing a relaxed climate conducive to good communication.  
   5 4 3 2 1

5. I make an effort to get the applicant to talk freely.  
   5 4 3 2 1

6. I use questions to draw out essential information.  
   5 4 3 2 1

7. I listen more than I talk.  
   5 4 3 2 1

8. I avoid preconception and personal bias.  
   5 4 3 2 1

9. I adhere to equal employment opportunity guidelines.  
   5 4 3 2 1

10. I record key points.  
    5 4 3 2 1

11. I provide information about the job and the organization and answer the applicant's questions.  
    5 4 3 2 1

12. I make selection decisions on the basis of job requirements.    5 4 3 2 1

13. I document my selection decisions.    5 4 3 2 1

14. I let all candidates know the outcome of their interview at the appropriate time.    5 4 3 2 1

TOTAL ———

A score between 56 and 70 suggests you probably conduct successful interviews. Scores between 42 and 55 indicate some significant strengths as well as some improvement needs. A score below 42 calls for a serious effort to improve. Make a special effort in any area where you scored 3 or less regardless of your total score.

# THE IMPORTANCE OF THE SELECTION INTERVIEW

The goal of each interview is to gather pertinent information in order to make the best possible decision about an applicant's ability to do a specific job. This information may include:

► Work experience

► Personal goals

► Education

► Evidence of dependability

► Technical, analytical, clerical, or manual skills and knowledge

► Attitude

► Hobbies and other interests

► Past achievements

► Interpersonal skills

► Ability to be a team player

Never underestimate the importance of the selection interview. The interview is the critical communications link in the selection process. It should meet the needs of the applicant as well as those of the hiring organization. The interviewer and the applicant will form important and lasting impressions of each other from the interview.

Applicants who appear reluctant to provide pertinent information about experience and skills are usually dismissed as serious candidates. Conversely, applicants' interest will be diminished by employers who seem unenthusiastic about the position and reluctant to talk about it and the organization.

Several aspects of the selection interview are described here. Each is vital to the goal of having a qualified trained staff that is focused on organizational goals and involved in their achievement.

### Getting Information

The interview must provide adequate information about the applicant's education, formal training, skills, work experience, performance in previous positions, plus personal characteristics (such as attitude, ability to communicate, etc.) This information will help you determine the interviewee's ability to do the job.

### Matching Individuals to Your Organization

Good performance in one organization does not automatically assure the same performance in another. The interview, therefore, must determine not only *if* the candidate can do the job, but also *whether* that person is anxious to perform it well in your organization.

### Giving Information

An applicant needs to learn basic job requirements plus other facts about your organization in order to make an intelligent decision. This information includes items such as: job description, hours of work, compensation, benefits coverage, and opportunities for personal growth.

Remember that the interview should promote good will between the candidate and your organization regardless of whether it ends with employment or not.

---

*Your Turn*

*Think these through:*

► How much interaction is expected between your new candidate and other members of your team? Would any personality characteristics be particularly welcome?

► Are any of your other employees experiencing difficulties in their present work function? How would that affect someone new?

---

# STAGES OF THE INTERVIEWING PROCESS

The process of interviewing falls into discrete stages. None of them can be skipped if you want to have the full benefit of an in-depth interview with your candidates.

## Planning

The first step in the interview is to gather information about the position. Discuss this with friends or employees if you need to. Ask them if it is clear, from what you've told them, what the job entails, what level of skills you require, and what benefits you have to offer.

Next look at each candidate's *personal qualifications* and write out any particular questions you would like that person to elaborate on—don't try and wing it. (You will learn more about how to ask questions in the next chapter of this book.) Remember, you want detailed information about how that particular candidate will function as a member of your team.

You will also have to prepare an environment which is comfortable for the interview and see that you not be disturbed during the process.

Prepare *yourself* by deciding to keep an open mind and not make snap judgments based on physical appearance or lack of skills in minor areas. Make sure you are familiar with equal opportunity laws.

## Conducting the Interview

You will learn more about designing and asking questions later, but for now remember that your goal is to give and take as much information as possible.

This is best done in an environment of open communication. If you are being honest, you can expect the same in return. Are there any difficult questions you feel you must pose to a specific candidate? Decide in advance diplomatic ways to phase them.

Also, think carefully about any information about the job you are reluctant to divulge. Why? Is there a problem in your organization that needs to be resolved? Decide whether it is unfair to keep certain issues from candidates—perhaps they will be able to offer solutions.

## Evaluating the Candidate

Before ending the interview, consult your notes and see if all vital areas (job skills, nature of the work day, structure of the organization, benefits) have all been covered. End the interview on a friendly note, whether or not you are impressed with the candidate.

Prior to putting your thoughts in writing, make a mental note of your overall impression of the candidate. Perhaps assign him or her a number from 1 to 10. After you have finished your evaluation, go back and see if this number has changed.

Begin your actual evaluation by looking at the job description itself. Check off each pertinent skill you feel the candidate possesses and note any failings. Are these trainable?

Next, consider the issue of how well you think that candidate fits your team. For instance, if the position requires a lot of customer support, is the candidate friendly and outgoing? Or is the individual so talkative as to disrupt other employees? Will the candidate have a sense of humor with irate customers or difficult colleagues? Is there deadline pressure or occasional overtime? Will that candidate pull his or her own weight?

Make sure your notations are in writing, so that you can come back to them later. Don't rely on memory only.

## Follow Up

Before ending the interview, establish and communicate a date upon which you will make your decision. Communicate in writing with the candidates, thanking each for the time and interest shown in responding to your vacancy. Take the extra step, if appropriate, of telling the candidate why they were not chosen (this should be as simple as letting them know that an extremely well-qualified candidate with direct experience was the one hired).

File your notes in an orderly fashion where you can access them quickly in the future.

# THE DYNAMICS OF INTERVIEWING

Schematically, the task of the interviewer looks like this:

| Positive Inputs | Positive Outcomes |
| --- | --- |
| Thorough preparation of job specifications. Interviewer prepares interview plan. | Candidates are selected or rejected for job-related reasons. |
| Interviewer probes for data in critical areas. Conclusions about candidate formed using appropriate data. Candidate qualifications measured against directly related job criteria. | Candidate feels his or her qualifications were fully presented. |
| Interviewer listens 80 percent of time. Candidate is expected to present pertinent data about experience, knowledge and values. | Candidate feels what he or she has to say is important. |
| Use of open-ended questions to stimulate the candidate. Questions are free of suggestions of bias or prejudice. The focus of the interview is consistently on the job. | Decisions are based on a broad range of pertinent data. Decisions are based on job-related facts, not whim or caprice. |
| Interviewer gives an honest description of the position, the organization, and related factors. Candidate has full opportunity to learn about position. | Candidate is properly prepared to make a decision concerning degree of interest in position. |

# BEFORE THE INTERVIEW: A REVIEW

After you have thoroughly studied the job specifications for the position you have available (covered in Chapter Three) you should prepare an action plan for each interview.

Study the applicant's general qualifications and work history from the employment application and/or resume. Determine what additional information, or clarification is required.

Decide what questions will fill any information gaps. Make a list of questions you want the applicant to answer. Keep these handy to insure they will not be overlooked during the interview. Be sure to include the "make" or "break" questions you plan to ask every candidate to assure consistency in evaluating qualifications against job requirements.

Review what information about the job and organization you will need to provide to the candidate. If you have an organizational chart or samples of your product (forms or documents, if you are in a service profession), make sure these are on hand.

Make sure you have gotten all necessary feedback from other employees since you will be asking the candidate to be a member of a team. If other team members will be involved in the selection process, make sure they will be available at the time of the interview.

# PROMOTING GOODWILL

An interview is essentially a social process and should be conducted accordingly. The tone should be pleasant, but businesslike. A good interview is designed to gain the cooperation and confidence of the interviewee. Professional interviewers do the following.

**Are on time.** This is just like any other business appointment. Have reading materials or coffee available if the candidate shows up early. Make sure someone is on hand to welcome the candidate.

**Treat applicants the same.** The way you greet and talk with applicants may be interpreted as a signal of good or ill will, and could invite charges of discrimination if your manner is inconsistent.

**Establish rapport.** Strive for a relaxed yet businesslike atmosphere conducive to open communication. Try to limit chat on personal affairs to just a few minutes. Introduce candidates to anyone else currently present in the office.

**Show respect for the individual.** Give each person your attention and listen to his or her views even though the candidate's value system may be different from your own. Show a genuine interest in the applicant.

**Provide information.** The candidate needs information on which to determine his or her interest in the job. Answer questions and, when appropriate, provide specific information about the job, working conditions, compensation, and benefits as well as the expectations and goals of your organization.

**Explain the placement process.** Don't leave people guessing. Tell them the purpose of the interview and what the next steps will be. Let them know when you expect to make a final decision.

## CLOSING THE INTERVIEW

Before you conclude the interview, it is essential the applicant's need for information be satisfied. In Chapter Three you learned how to adequately assess the job and the organization. This includes specific job requirements, working hours, starting date, salary and benefits, as well as something about the organization, and its people.

The best time to discuss these items in any detail is toward the *end of the interview*. One reason for this is because the interviewer wants an applicant's responses to questions to be unbiased and spontaneous—not influenced by what the applicant thinks he or she wants to hear. Some candidates are adept at saying exactly what the interviewer has unknowingly coached them to say.

As soon as both parties have the information they need, the interviewer should bring the interview to a close. An excellent way to accomplish this is when the interviewer:

1. Assesses the applicant's interest in the position.

2. Informs the applicant where things stand and what the next steps will be.

3. Insures the candidate understands when a decision will be made and how he or she will be notified.

4. Thanks the interviewee for his or her time and closes the session on a positive note.

Remember to follow through! Every applicant deserves an answer as soon as it can be provided.

## Remember Your Goals

If the people you select to be on your team are not successful, you will not be successful. Human resources are the most critical part of any organization's success. A good staff ensures profitability, productivity, growth and long-term survival. You simply cannot survive without qualified people. As a team leader it is essential these people learn to work together.

# ASK YOURSELF

► Do you analyze job requirements thoroughly before beginning the selection process?

► Do you always look for objective evidence of an applicant's skills, knowledge, past successes and failures, dependability, and attitude toward work, coworkers, supervision, and customers?

► Do you describe your idea of teamwork to applicants and ask them to assess how they would work under team conditions?

► Do you make sure each applicant understands the job requirements and expected standards of performance?

► Do you evaluate facts carefully and avoid making premature conclusions or stereotyping while making a selection decision?

# CHAPTER FIVE

# QUESTIONING SKILLS

## DEVELOP-ING YOUR QUESTION-ING SKILLS

Questioning skills are very important. A candidate's willingness to share information is often directly proportionate to the questioning skill of the interviewer. In this chapter, you will learn how to apply these skills.

## Questions That Yield Information

The sample questions in the previous section have a major characteristic in common—they *open up* information channels rather than close them.

The best questions open up information channels and employ the words *who, what, where, when,* and *how.* Try to avoid questions that can be answered with a simple "yes" or "no." Compare "What were your sales like at your last company?" to "Were your sales good at the last company?" Note how the first leads to a description of vital information while the second leaves you guessing as to what "yes" or "no" might mean.

As you practice with "who, what, where, when, and how" questions, think about how precise an answer you need to each question. You don't want candidates to be overly vague either. Start thinking in terms of *directive* versus *nondirective* questions.

### Nondirective Questions

Nondirective questions are those that encourage applicants to express goals, values, qualifications, and feelings. These are also sometimes called *open-ended questions.* Here is an example: "What led to your decision to leave your last job?" Nondirective questions are especially useful in obtaining *subjective* or *personal information* from the candidate. They are also helpful when the candidate appears to be holding back or providing guarded replies.

### Directive Questions

In contrast, directive questions are used to gather data that is *factual* and *objective.* Directive questions do not probe an applicant's values or ideas. "When could you begin work if hired?" is a directive question. Another example is, "What was your starting salary at your previous company?"

### Nondirective and Directive

Questions can be used together to solicit an individual's general background, and then focus on a specific aspect. Here is an example:

| | |
|---|---|
| *Nondirective question:* | What personal qualities contribute to your success as an engineer? |
| *Directive question:* | How many engineering projects did you supervise last year? |
| *Nondirective question:* | How did you get along with your last supervisor? |
| *Directive question:* | What references from former employers can you furnish? |

## Practicing with Questions

Complete the exercise below by creating one nondirective and one directive question for each area of interest.

| Areas to Be Explored | Nondirective Question | Directive Question |
|---|---|---|
| *Previous Employment* | | |
| *College or University* | | |
| *Interest in the Position* | | |
| *Unique Qualifications* | | |
| *Personal Goals* | | |

# Response to Practicing with Questions

Compare your answers to the samples given here.

| Areas to Be Explored | Nondirective Question | Directive Question |
| --- | --- | --- |
| *Previous Employment* | Why do you think you were so successful in your last job? | When did you get your last salary increase? |
| *College or University* | Why did you elect to major in math? | What was your grade point average? |
| *Interest in the Position* | How did you happen to become interested in this job? | Does this job appeal to you enough to start at a lower salary? |
| *Unique Qualifications* | What qualifications do you feel you have that uniquely qualify you for this position? | Can you give me two unique qualifications you would bring to this job? |
| *Personal Goals* | What goals have you set for yourself for the next two or three years? | Which goal do you expect to attain first? |

# USING PROBES IN AN INTERVIEW

*Probes* are used to gain *additional* or *clearer* information from a candidate. This section will teach you various probing techniques.

The simpler techniques, such as silence or uttering an occasional "uh-huh," encourage the candidate to keep talking. (Remember, the candidate should do more talking than the interviewer!)

The more aggressive techniques are helpful in honing in on a response that is too vague. If you suspect that a candidate is guarded or deceptive, these techniques will help you bring that out in the open.

# Probing Techniques

Here are some examples of commonly used probes:

| Probe | Purpose or Technique | Example (Interviewer's response in boldface) |
|-------|----------------------|----------------------------------------------|
| **Silence** | The interviewer looks expectantly at the applicant but does not speak. | "You know . . . I think they took advantage of me?" **Silence—5 to 10 seconds.** "Yeah, they promised me a promotion but I never got it." |
| **Neutral response** | An expression by the interviewer to encourage more information without biasing it. | "It sounded good at the time," **"Uh-huh."** "It didn't turn out that way though." **"Could you explain what you mean?"** |
| **Clarifying** | An attempt to determine the meaning of a response. | "A person who is not part of the 'in' group can't expect an increase." **"What do you mean by 'in' group?"** |
| **Expanding** | Seeking new information to build on a previous statement. | "I was beginning to pick up vibrations that my job might be phased out." **"Oh, yes? What vibrations?"** |
| **Confirming feelings** | A reflection by the interviewer expressing what he or she believes the applicant's intended meaning to be. | "I didn't get any credit for the new system even though it was my idea and I worked over 1,000 hours on it." **"You feel your creativity and willingness to work long hours were not appreciated?"** |

| Probe | Purpose or Technique | Example (Interviewer's response in boldface) |
|---|---|---|
| **Summarizing key ideas** | An effort by the interviewer to summarize the last few applicant responses. | "So basically it was my baby all the way." **"It was your idea, you sold it to top management, and then worked out all the details, including implementation. Right?"** |
| **Repeating** | Persisting in getting an answer to the question already asked but not answered. | "Which of your qualifications contributed to your promotion?" **"Well, you see the old supervisor retired so the job was open."** "I see, but which of your qualifications contributed to your promotion?" |
| **Clarifying inconsistencies** | Reflecting that what the applicant has just said is inconsistent with a previous statement. | "That being the case, I decided to look for another job." **"I'm sorry, I seem to be confused. I thought you left that job to finish analytical training. What gave me that impression?"** |

# CASE STUDY

## The Silent Candidate

Jackson Towne is establishing his own public accounting firm and has just conducted his first interview to fill a key position. The candidate, Joan Smith, seemed well qualified on paper but had so little to say during the interview that Jackson is concerned about her ability to communicate with other employees and clients in the normal course of business.

Joan answered most of his questions with a simple "yes" or "no." She seemed impressed when he told her about his extensive background and accomplishments, but did not offer to share her own. She became flustered when he criticized the quality of the accounting curriculum at the college she attended, but did not challenge his remarks. In fact, she became even quieter by the end of the interview.

Why do you think the applicant remained silent? (*Note:* more than one reason may account for such behavior.)

❏ Joan Smith was shy.

❏ Her verbal skills were weak.

❏ She was intimidated by Jackson Towne.

❏ She wasn't feeling well.

❏ The questions Jackson Towne asked lent themselves to "yes" or "no" answers rather than a free flow of information.

## Response to Case Study

The applicant appears to have been intimidated by Jackson Towne's approach to the interview, and his desire to impress her with his own qualifications.

Questions that can be answered only "yes" or "no" are the *responsibility of the interviewer* and will not encourage employees to elaborate their answers. Jackson should strive to be less intimidating and learn to use questions to his advantage. Joan, in turn, may have to develop a little more self-assertion.

# USING PROBES TO GATHER JOB-RELATED DATA

An interviewer needs to determine how a candidate will function in everyday job activities. Methods to gather this information must be job centered and pursued without discriminatory overtones. Questions should stimulate the applicant to respond naturally. In this section, the probing techniques you just learned are illustrated at more length. Notice how they elicit precise job information while retaining a friendly tone.

### Ask general, open-ended questions that do not suggest a particular answer.

"Could you tell me a little about how you got that promotion?" will tell you more about what the person considers important than "Do you like your job?" Another useful open-ended technique is to follow an answer with "What happened then?" or "What did you do next?"

### Use short questions.

The more words you use in a question, the more likely you are to influence the answer. If the applicant says, "I thought the group I worked with was excellent," you might say, "What made the group in which you worked excellent?" A better response would be "In what sense?" or "How so?" The applicant is more apt to react in a normal way since there is nothing in the question that requires evaluation or suggests a particular response. Spontaneity often yields what an applicant *really feels*.

### Listen carefully to each response; then decide on your next question.

An interviewer learns more from listening than talking! A good interviewer spends nearly 80 percent of the time listening. Many inexperienced interviewers are in such a hurry to get to the next question, they fail to hear the applicant's response. Listen attentively to each answer. Often an answer will determine the next question. If the response does not provide enough information, say "tell me more" or "can you be more specific?" If the information is adequate for the question being asked, go on with the interview plan.

### Probe the candidate's range of expertise.

Ask applicants basic, fundamental questions about their field of expertise. Interviewers should not try to demonstrate equal or superior knowledge to a candidate (even if they possess it). The best responses are given freely and normally. Those which are guarded or tentative because an applicant fears the level of the interviewer's expertise will be difficult to evaluate.

### Stimulate value judgments.

Asking a candidate how he or she feels about punctuality, conduct on the job, or personal commitment to a task or relationships with previous co-workers will help provide insights in that person's value system. This information is more valuable when evaluating a candidate than an interviewer's "assumptions."

### Probe "choice points."

"Choice points" are situations which require the applicant to explain why one course of action was selected over another. For example, why the candidate majored in business instead of engineering. Listening to reasons why a choice was made can help provide insights to the individual's reasoning and value system.

### Use silence effectively.

Some interviewers become uncomfortable when silence occurs during an interview and feel compelled to talk. Silence provides time to think (which is often what the applicant is doing). Interviewers who wait out the silence while looking expectantly at the interviewee will learn more than those who don't. An applicant, sensing more information is desired, will often provide more pertinent information than anticipated.

## Use reflective statements.

Reflecting comments back to a candidate is a good technique. It shows you were listening and wish to stimulate elaboration of an answer. This must be done in a natural way which shows interest or concern. Here is an example:

APPLICANT: I was pretty excited over the special assignment!

INTERVIEWER: You were pretty excited about the project?

APPLICANT: Sure, it was the one I had worked to achieve and one I felt I had earned.

INTERVIEWER: You felt you had earned it?

APPLICANT: I went to school for six months at night to qualify.

INTERVIEWER: Six months?

APPLICANT: That's right. Three nights a week and three hours a night.

---

*Your Turn*     **Please answer the following true-false questions.**

|  | True | False |
|---|---|---|
| 1. It is a good idea to spend ten to fifteen minutes establishing rapport. | ☐ | ☐ |
| 2. The interviewer should be listening about eighty percent of the time. | ☐ | ☐ |
| 3. You should handle reluctant candidates by asking pointed questions. | ☐ | ☐ |
| 4. Asking questions that can be answered "yes" or "no" saves time and makes evaluation easier. | ☐ | ☐ |
| 5. When making a selection decision, judge candidates on job qualifications, not on "liking" one more than another. | ☐ | ☐ |

6. All applicants need to know when they will be notified of the outcome of the interview. ☐ ☐

7. The interviewer should take brief notes on key points. ☐ ☐

8. Rejected applicants should be told why in detail. ☐ ☐

9. The applicant's skills are very important but so are attitudes, motivation, and values. ☐ ☐

10. How you document your selection decision is important. ☐ ☐

*Now compare your answers with those of the author.*

## Your Turn Answers

1. *False.* Rapport can be established in five minutes or less.

2. *True.* How else can you acquire the information you need?

3. *True.* Probes help you with evasive, vague, or sketchy replies.

4. *False.* "Yes" and "no" answers may save time but they make evaluation impossible.

5. *True.* Job qualifications count the most.

6. *True.* Applicants also need to make plans and consider options.

7. *True.* Notes are helpful in evaluating candidates.

8. *False.* Tell them "the best qualified applicant was selected."

9. *True.* Skills are essential but the person must also want to apply them.

10. *True.* It may make the difference in winning or losing a discrimination complaint.

# Job-Related Questions

A variety of job-related questions are listed below. You may find some of these questions (or variations of them) helpful in obtaining information from applicants.

1. **Questions to Learn How the Applicant Regards Current or Past Positions.**

   - Would you tell me about your present (last) position?

   - How would you describe a typical work day?

   - What activities did you enjoy most at your last job?

   - What do you feel you do best? Why?

   - What job functions are the most difficult for you? Why?

   - What was your greatest contribution in your present (past) position?

   - How have you improved your position from the one you originally accepted?

   - What are the reasons you left your last job?

2. **Questions to Probe the Applicant's Relationships with People.**

   - How would you describe your supervisor?

   - What do you feel are your supervisor's greatest strengths? Why? Weaknesses? Why?

   - In what ways has your supervisor supported your performance?

   - For what kinds of things have you been praised? Criticized?

   - How would you characterize your co-workers?

   - What disagreements have you had with co-workers?

   - What kind of people do you enjoy working with? What kind do you find difficult?

- What do you consider essential in the management of people?
- What type of committees have you worked on? What did you contribute?

3. **Questions to Explore Aspirations.**

   - What is important to you in a job? What would you like to avoid?
   - What do you want from this job that is lacking in your present (past) one?
   - What position do you expect to hold five years from now?
   - What are you doing to achieve your career goals?
   - What are your salary expectations? On what do you base them?

4. **Questions to Stimulate Self-Assessment.**

   - As an employee, what do you consider your greatest strength?
   - In what areas would you most like to improve? Why?
   - What motivates you?
   - Why did you select this particular field of work?

5. **Questions to Determine How the Applicant Would Apply Skills, Experience and Knowledge to the Vacant Position.**

   - What attracts you to the job for which you are applying?
   - What do you believe qualifies you for this position?
   - What elements of this job would be new to you?
   - What additional training do you feel is required to achieve full proficiency?

Keep these job-related questions handy as you prepare to interview candidates. In fact, you might like to photocopy a sheet for each candidate and check off all those questions you want to be sure to ask.

---

*Your Turn*

***Think about the material you have read.***

▶ What did you learn about interviewing and the selection process?

▶ What did you learn about yourself?

▶ How can you apply what you learned?

***Answer the following questions.***

▶ My current interviewing and evaluation skills are effective in the following areas.

▶ I need to improve my interviewing and evaluation skills in the following areas.

▶ My interviewing and evaluation skills improvement goals are as follows. (Be sure they are specific, attainable, and measurable.)

▶ I have developed action steps, along with a timetable to accomplish each goal.

---

# ASK YOURSELF

▶ How do you divide your talking and listening time when you are interviewing an applicant?

▶ Do you conclude an interview with enough insight into a candidate's experience to make a well-considered employment decision?

▶ What is your ratio of employment successes to failures? Are you satisfied with it? How can you improve it?

▶ Can you name two improvements you need to make in the selection process personally?

CHAPTER
SIX

# MAKING THE EVALUATION AND LEGAL COMPLIANCE

CHAPTER SIX

# EVALUATING CANDIDATES

Following the interview, the applicant's qualifications must be objectively evaluated in terms of the position to be filled. Can the applicant do the job? Will the candidate make a positive contribution to the hiring organization? Four general principles govern evaluation. They include:

### Be Hypercritical

The decision to hire is one of the most important decisions an organization will face. A poor decision will be expensive and painful to everyone concerned.

Do not gloss over any basic weakness because you like some other less important qualification. If you notice a job-related weakness (such as poor verbal skills in a customer relations applicant) during the interview, think how difficult it will be to live with once the person has been hired and is not nearly so anxious to please.

### Base Your Evaluation on Facts

Compare qualifications against job requirements. Do not look for, or guess at, hidden meanings in the individual's responses or behavior. Be aware of behaviors that are likely to surface once on the job.

### Concentrate on Behavior, Not Words Alone

Some interviewers are carried away by the applicant's words and overlook behavior. If a candidate is asked to describe his or her former supervisor, for example, there is no way of knowing how accurate that description is. What the applicant emphasizes, however, can be important. An observer can learn much about the applicant's likes and dislikes, organizational skills, and general attitude by concentrating on both words *and* behavior.

### Seek Confirmation of Your Evaluation

Check your evaluation with other interviewers who talked to the same person. Check academic credentials with the granting institution. Talk to at least two previous employers. If references are listed, call them.

# MAINTAINING OBJECTIVITY

Objectivity is an essential quality when evaluating an applicant.

For example, disabled people often produce more high quality work than their nondisabled colleagues. Older employees are frequently more reliable, productive and loyal than those who are younger. Be sure you are evaluating the right things!

There are several ways to maintain objectivity when evaluating prospective employees. They include the following.

1. Evaluate the extent of the applicant's experience and the effectiveness of past performance against your job requirements. Are both acceptable? Try to remember that ten years' of experience is quite different from one year of experience ten times. Focus on what was accomplished in past jobs.

2. Determine the level of responsibility previously held by the applicant. Is it about the same? More? Less? Can the applicant make the transition to the position in question?

3. Examine the skill and knowledge level of the applicant. Are they adequate to meet your needs? Are they adaptable to your job?

4. Identify the applicant's strengths. Are they adaptable? Will they enhance the position in question?

5. Determine the applicant's weaknesses. Would they have a negative effect on performance or be inconsequential?

6. Evaluate indicators of stability and progress. Can you reasonably project the future based on the past record? Are stability and progress important to the job?

7. Will the applicant be compatible with others in the work group?

8. Probe the history of the candidate to determine past dependability, productivity, and attitude toward work, co-workers, supervision, and customers.

9. Check all references carefully. In addition, verify all dates of employment, jobs held, academic institutions attended, degrees conferred, and special honors awarded.

## Making Rational Decisions

Most people have prejudices. Interviewers must recognize theirs, and neutralize them during a job interview.

Physical appearance, clothing, and personal mannerisms often play too large a role in the selection of a candidate. Guard against having one negative aspect cause you to overlook the positives. Similarly do not allow one positive aspect to blind you to the negatives.

It is important to:

▶ Evaluate all applicants by the same criteria

▶ Be aware of your equal opportunity goals

▶ Not violate federal, state or local laws

▶ Give all candidates the same consideration

Try to compare applicants to the job—not one against the other. Use the Comparison of Candidates to Position Requirements approach illustrated on the next page.

*Your Turn*     *Answer these questions.*

▶ How many incorrect employment decisions can your business tolerate before it begins to show in the bottom line?

▶ List the positions in your organization that have the most critical impact on its success.

▶ Now list the requirements of each of those positions that are critical to success. Do the current incumbents fulfill those requirements?

# Comparison of Candidates to Position Requirements

POSITION TO BE FILLED: <u>**Administrator/Community Health Education**</u>

Rate each candidate using the following scale.

1. Knowledge and/or skill level well below position requirements.
2. Knowledge and/or skill level meet minimum position requirements.
3. Knowledge and/or skill level meet all position requirements.
4. Knowledge and/or skill level unusually extensive and useful in this position.
5. Knowledge and/or skill level exceed position requirements.

Circle the name of the candidate selected.

| | CANDIDATES | | | |
|---|---|---|---|---|
| | *S. G.* *Jerome* | *P. R.* *Parker* | *N. S.* *Sherman* | *A. P.* *Norman* |
| | RANKING | | | |
| General Knowledge Requirements: | | | | |
| 1. *Community Health Education Functions* | *1* | *2* | *4* | *2* |
| 2. | | | | |
| 3. | | | | |
| 4. | | | | |
| Specific Job Skills and/or Knowledge: | | | | |
| 1. *Typing—55 wpm* | *3* | *3* | *3* | *3* |
| 2. *Spelling & Grammar* | *2* | *3* | *3* | *3* |
| 3. *Basic Math Skills* | *1* | *3* | *4* | *2* |
| 4. *Page layout* | *3* | *3* | *4* | *3* |
| Administrative Skills and/or Knowledge: | | | | |
| 1. *Filing & Filing Systems* | *2* | *3* | *4* | *3* |
| 2. *Office Machines* | *2* | *3* | *3* | *3* |
| 3. *Office Procedure & Practice* | *2* | *3* | *4* | *3* |
| 4. | | | | |
| Attitude | *3* | *3* | *4* | *4* |
| TOTALS | *19* | *26* | *33* | *26* |

# COMPLYING WITH EQUAL OPPORTUNITY LAWS

An interviewer must be able to demonstrate that all candidates for a position were evaluated on the same basis, and also show that the criteria used were directly job related. If supporting documentation cannot be produced, discrimination complaints may be impossible to defend.

You should familiarize the appropriate employees with the basic elements of labor law, including equal employment opportunity, that they need to know. You should also make sure your places of business are properly posted with required legal notices to employees.

Remember when using questions that the questions should be directed to determine work related skills. Questions that could be construed to be discriminatory such as questions on race, color, national origin, sex, religion, age, or disability should be avoided.

Note that you should let all candidates know the status of their application as soon as possible. Those not employed may be told, "The candidate whose qualifications best fit the job specifications was selected."

## Documenting the Selection Process

A form similar to the following Application Form can be useful in documenting decisions. It should be supported by an accurate set of job specifications to which the applicant's qualifications have been compared.

This form helps demonstrate adherence to equal employment opportunity guidelines by documenting the reasons the decision was made to employ or reject a candidate. Such decisions must be based on valid, directly related job criteria applied consistently to all candidates.

# Candidate Disposition

CANDIDATE: *S. G. Jerome*

POSITION APPLIED FOR: **Administrative Assistant/Community Health Education**

DATE: **11/30**

Job offer will ( ) will not (✔) be extended.

1. Does not meet minimum job specifications.

2. Meets minimum specifications, but not best qualified.

3. No prior related experience.

4. Less prior related experience than person selected.

5. Cannot meet physical standards for the position.

6. Lower level of required skills than person selected.

7. Less directly related training than candidate chosen.

8. Cannot work the schedule or hours required.

9. Applicant withdrew from consideration.

10. Other (list job-related reason): _____

_____

Job-related reason candidate selected was best qualified:

**Four years directly related experience in a comparable community health education position.**

Directly job-related reason this candidate was not selected. Insert appropriate number from the list above: **4**

# ILLEGAL EMPLOYMENT PRACTICES

Legislation covering equal employment opportunity is extensive and complex. Therefore, only the basics of unlawful selection practices can be highlighted here. Copies of Local, State, and Federal laws can be obtained from the appropriate governmental agency.

The following practices reflect the thrust of current legislation.

**UNDER CURRENT LEGISLATION IT IS UNLAWFUL TO:**

1. Refuse to consider for employment, or otherwise discriminate against any person because of race, color, national origin, sex, religion, physical disability or age.

2. Show a bias in help-wanted advertising for or against applicants unless you can prove your requirements are bonafide occupational qualifications.

3. Use any screening techniques for employment or promotion, i.e., paper and pencil tests, questionnaires, etc., that cannot be proved to be directly job related.

4. Categorize job candidates on the basis of race, color, national origin, sex, religion or age.

5. Ask about previous mental and physical disabilities during an interview.

6. Refuse to hire a woman because separate facilities would have to be provided. Nor can an employer refuse to hire a woman because he would have to pay her special benefits, i.e., premium overtime, rest periods, etc., required by State law.

7. Perpetuate past discriminatory practices that have led to statistical imbalances in the workforce.

8. Use polygraphs, voice print devices and other related technology in the selection of employees.

9. Seek facts that may indirectly reveal the applicant's race, color, religion or national origin.

10. Request information about police or arrest records that have not resulted in convictions.

# ASK YOURSELF

▶ Are the employees who are doing your recruiting and selection familiar with the basic tenets of equal employment opportunity legislation?

▶ What would be the cost of litigation and a judgment against your company because of an equal employment opportunity violation?

▶ Are any of those making selection decisions using any kinds of testing in making their decisions (especially those they have devised themselves)? How do you assess the value of these tools?

# CHAPTER
# SEVEN

# ENCOURAGING
# INVOLVEMENT
# AND
# DEVELOPMENT

CHAPTER SEVEN

## MANAGERS' IMPACT ON COMMIT-MENT

How involved an employee feels is greatly influenced by the attitude of the team leader. Individuals must feel that their contributions are valued; otherwise, they will only participate to a minimal level. Following are several management styles; which fits you the most?

**"I know best."** This person feels work should be done by controlling the people who do it. Employees are told what to do, how to do it, and when to stop. Then they are told what they did wrong and what they did right; where they are weak, and where they are strong. The person in charge feels this is justified because of his or her superior knowledge and ability. This attitude does not invite new ideas, challenge people, or stimulate a cooperative, supportive spirit. Communication is directed one way only.

**"I'll set the goals, you meet them."** This person feels that because of his or her superior knowledge, ability, or experience it is okay to establish goals for others to meet. The employee is given an opportunity to discuss ways to meet goals, but has no input into the actual performance objectives. When this happens commitment is more difficult to obtain from employees because their lack of involvement precludes a sense of ownership.

**"Let's review the work together, establish realistic goals, and evaluate performance accordingly."** This leader emphasizes work performance, not authoritarian control. The idea is to first communicate organizational needs, then help team members contribute their ideas. The leader acts as a resource and enabler rather than as a judge. Communication is open and flows in both directions. The value of mutual support and cooperation is recognized and employed.

## MAKING COMMITMENT POSSIBLE

Commitment cannot be forced. It is self-generating and usually develops through a feeling of involvement. People increase commitment to a team when they are allowed to contribute to its success. Once actively involved in goal setting and problem solving, a sense of ownership is developed. Team goals can be effectively pursued, much like an entrepreneur. Employees feel more important (and needed) when they feel a responsibility for results. This is the time a genuine concern is developed for other team members. Group problems become individual problems, and team goals become individual goals. Members contribute their best to problem solving because they have a personal stake in doing so.

When members help design the systems and methods used by the team, they understand why controls are important and make a commitment to support them. This is especially true when they know it is possible to revise or improve controls when required.

Involvement also helps team members satisfy the participative needs of others. It helps build a framework in which individual member needs can be learned, understood, and supported by all.

Owners cannot do it all, no matter how talented and committed they may be. Their success depends on their ability to delegate intelligently and then motivate employees to accomplish the goals of the organization. The highest level of achievement is attained when a team is committed to the task and full use is made of each member's talents.

A supervisor controls the degree to which employees are involved. He or she also opens up opportunities for participation and watches the commitment grow.

# INVOLVING TEAM MEMBERS

A *goal* is a statement of results to be achieved. Goals describe: (1) conditions that will exist when the desired outcome has been accomplished, (2) a time frame during which the outcome is to be completed, and (3) resources the organization is willing to commit to achieve the desired result.

A *standard* refers to an ongoing performance criteria that must be met time and again. Standards are usually expressed quantitatively, and refer to such things as attendance, breakage, manufacturing tolerances, production rates, and safety standards.

Goals and standards should be challenging, but achievable. They should be established with the participation of those responsible for meeting them. After all, well-selected and trained employees should know more about what is achievable than anyone else.

Here is one way team members can help establish goals and standards and the action plans necessary to achieve them. Like other critical skills, goal setting may take practice.

The role of the team member and the team leader are outlined on page 88.

These roles place the responsibility for performance on the appropriate team members and provide the latitude to achieve results. The leader concentrates on being a challenger, prober, coach, and enabler.

| Team Member | Team Leader |
|---|---|
| Helps establish performance goals and standards. This is a "self-contract" for achievement as well as a commitment to deliver a result for the team. | Ensures team goals are achievable, but challenging enough to meet organizational needs and provide a sense of accomplishment. |
| Develops methods to measure results and checkpoints for control purposes. | Helps balance the complexity of measures and controls with value received. |
| Outlines the action required to accomplish goals and standards. | Participates with the team to test the action plan's validity against other alternatives. |
| Specifies participation required from colleagues or in other units within the organization. | Reviews what cooperation and support is required and helps obtain it if required. |
| Reports progress as work is performed. Seeks guidance and assistance when needed. Adjusts plan as required. | Follows the progress of the work. Reinforces achievement and assists in problem solving when indicated. Ensures targets are met or modified if circumstances so indicate. |

*Your Turn*

*Answer the following:*

► Outline the process of setting goals and standards in your company. Can it be improved?

► Who takes the lead in solving problems in your company?

► Does problem solving in your company concentrate on finding out who is at fault or on solving the problem and preventing its reoccurrence?

► How do you rate yourself in terms of being able to get your employees involved and in developing a sense of ownership?

# DEVELOPING EFFECTIVE TEAM MEMBERS

Well-trained employees have confidence in their ability to contribute to the team effort. They understand why it is important to help support other members of the team.

Resources such as knowledge of the needs of the organization and control of work assignments are often available only to supervisors.

Any owner interested in improving team performance will insure training for each team member as appropriate.

## Trained Employees Can Help Solve Problems

Involved and well-trained team members can be highly helpful in solving problems. In fact, getting employees involved means passing along ownership of problems that rightfully belong to them.

Many owners spend too much time solving problems that could be better handled by employees. When owners feel responsible for solving all the problems, production is slowed, employees are frustrated, and personal growth is limited. The owner ends up with less time to plan, organize, motivate, and control.

Team effectiveness is more easily achieved when the owner simply participates in problem solving rather than dominating it.

# PROVIDING OPPORTUNITIES FOR GROWTH

Do you attempt to build new employee skills and strengthen existing ones? Do you prepare people properly for assignments you wish to delegate to them? Your attitude, knowledge, and approach will influence what is learned and how well it is applied. Here are some suggestions to improve the return on investment in training for all concerned.

► Review performance against expectations with each employee, and jointly identify training that will strengthen results.

► Listen to employees' growth objectives and support them through delegation when possible.

► Talk in advance to employees selected for training to emphasize the importance of the training to their job and their delegated assignments.

► Have an employee's work covered by others while that employee is in formal training, so he or she can concentrate on what is being taught.

► Help employees develop an action plan to apply their training to the job and to any additional assignments delegated.

► Ask the employees for an evaluation of the training program and whether it would be suitable for other members of the team.

► Delegate work to employees that allows them to apply new techniques and methods learned during training.

► Compliment employees when they apply their newly acquired skills.

Remember, qualified employees are receptive to delegation and the growth opportunities it provides.

# CASE STUDY

## The Complaining Employees

Marla and Sue work in computer services under the supervision of Janice Johns. They are both depressed about their jobs and have been complaining to one another. Marla is unhappy because she has never seen a description of her job and has only a limited understanding of what is expected of her. When she asked Janice about it, she was told, "Don't worry, I'll keep you busy." Marla never receives a new assignment until she completes the previous one she was assigned. Sometimes a day or more will pass before Janice is able to give Marla a new project. Recently Marla started helping a co-worker because she had nothing else to do. Janice later told her: "Don't do that again. Assignment of the work is my responsibility." Marla has since been criticized by her co-workers for not pitching in when they are busy and she is not.

Sue, on the other hand, is concerned about the backlog building up in her job. The problem occurred because of repeated changes in project objectives which were not communicated until after a critical point in the work had been passed. Janice insists on personally handling all communications with other groups serviced by their department. Because Janice is so busy, she frequently fails to pass important information along to Sue and is equally slow in getting answers from Sue which are needed by others.

Are Sue's and Marla's complaints justified? _____

Support your position:

_____

_____

_____

_____

_____

_____

# Response to Case Study

Marla and Sue have good reason to complain. Marla wants the opportunity to grow beyond her current tasks. Her efforts to learn what is expected of her have been blocked, and she is discouraged by waiting for assignments. She has been told not to worry about being idle and counseled not to help others unless directed to do so. This is frustrating for people who want to contribute.

Sue is suffering the consequences of poor communication from her supervisor. This is an impossible situation for Sue to correct until Janice either opens communication channels between users and Sue, or begins relaying information in a timely manner.

Janice appears to be over-controlling her employees by assuming they cannot think for themselves. She is also preventing voluntary attempts by employees to help and support one another. Janice needs to re-evaluate her approach to supervision and be more open in her dealings with employees. Otherwise, Janice will soon be an "ex-manager."

# ASK YOURSELF

► Have you examined the various functions performed within your business to determine where either formal or informal training of personnel would impact the bottom line? What about interaction with customers, suppliers and between employees? Could productivity be improved through better time management? Do employees understand the importance of quality in terms of product, initial sales, repeat business, and delivery?

► Have you set aside a portion of your budget to support employee training and development?

► Do you have a results oriented employee evaluation system that will help identify training needs?

► Have you tried to identify employees who have the expertise, ability, and desire to develop others?

► Have you ever made a comparison between the cost of an employee mistake and the cost of the training that would have prevented it?

CHAPTER SEVEN

# CHAPTER EIGHT

# BUILDING COLLABORATION, COMMUNICATION AND TRUST

CHAPTER EIGHT

## DEVELOP-ING SOURCES OF POWER

Once you have a qualified staff, properly trained and focused on organizational goals, you have accomplished a great deal.

But now you must concentrate on building an atmosphere conducive to open communication, cooperation and trust not only within your team, but also between your team and your customers.

Bringing team members together to collaborate on projects of mutual interest and to generate ideas and suggestions for improvement of productivity is one way to do this.

## THE BENEFITS OF COLLABORATION

Collaboration has many benefits when it is used well. In the list below, identify those advantages of importance to you.

- ► Collaboration builds an awareness of interdependence. When people recognize the benefits of helping one another, and realize it is expected, they will work together to achieve common goals. The effort is non-threatening.

- ► When people work together to achieve common goals, they stimulate each other to higher levels of accomplishment. Fresh ideas are generated and tested, and the team's productivity exceeds any combined efforts of employees working individually.

- ► Collaboration builds and reinforces recognition and mutual support within a team. People have an opportunity to see the effect of their effort and the efforts of others on achievement.

- ► Collaboration leads to the commitment to support and accomplish organizational goals. People gain personal power in the form of confidence when they know others share their views and are acting in concert with them.

## How to Achieve Collaboration

The benefits of collaboration make it easy to understand why managers who can make it happen are considered leaders. Collaboration can be encouraged and supported in the following ways.

► Identify areas of interdependence that make collaboration appropriate. Involve team members in planning and problem solving to help them identify where collaboration is needed.

► Keep lines of communication open between everyone involved in a problem, project, or course of action.

► Let the team know in advance that teamwork will positively influence individual recognition.

# FACILITATING OPEN COMMUNICATION

A leader uses communication to gather, process, and transmit information essential to the wellbeing of the organization. Since this communication moves in many directions, leaders must carefully consider the needs of peers, customers, and team members.

The team leader can often facilitate communications by responding to the information needs of the organization. A good starting place to identify these information needs is to ask yourself the questions in the chart on page 99.

 *Your Turn*

*Ask yourself the following:*

► How many times have customer complaints occurred because of internal communication errors?

► What aspects of your business are most critically affected by communication errors? Have you established safeguards?

► Ask yourself which of the functional areas of your business would have the greatest decline in productivity if the employees did not collaborate effectively?

| | Information From: | Information To: |
|---|---|---|
| **Customers** | What information do I need from my customers? | What information should I provide my customers? |
| | Where should I get it? | How should it be conveyed? |
| | When should I get it? | How often is it required? |
| | | When should I send it? |
| **Employees** | What information should I get from people working for me? | What do employees working for me want to know? |
| | How should I get it? | How do I provide it? |
| | How often? | When do I get someone else to provide it? |
| | What should I do with it? | |

# GOOD COMMUNICATION LEADS TO BETTER PRODUCTIVITY

Research shows the best leaders are good communicators. They have learned to give clear instructions, stay responsive to questions and suggestions, and keep the appropriate parties well informed.

Research also confirms a positive correlation between communication (understanding) and:

► Improved productivity

► Better problem solving

► A reduction in grievances

► Ideas for improvement in methodology

► Improved working relationships

► Greater personal satisfaction

## Test Your Communication Skills

Complete each of the following statements by circling the most appropriate choice.

1. Messages are the most easily understood when:

   (a) you use your full command of the language.

   (b) they are sent in terms the receiver understands.

2. Complex information is more easily understood when you:

   (a) improve clarity by using specific examples and analogies.

   (b) tell the listener to pay careful attention.

3. Key concepts are better remembered when you:

   (a) use repetition to reinforce them.

   (b) express yourself clearly.

4. Organizing a message before transmitting it:

   (a) often takes more time than it is worth.

   (b) makes it easier to understand.

5. The sender can determine the receiver's understanding by:

   (a) asking if he or she understands.

   (b) asking the receiver to report what he or she heard.

6. Listening is more effective when you:

   (a) concentrate on the sender and what is being said.

   (b) anticipate what the speaker is going to say.

7. Understanding is easier when you:

   (a) suspend judgment until the sender finishes the message.

   (b) assume you know the sender's position and respond quickly.

8. Understanding can be improved by the listener:

   (a) periodically paraphrasing the message back to the sender.

   (b) interrupting to express feelings and emotions.

9. Good listeners:

   (a) have their response ready when the sender stops talking.

   (b) ask questions when they don't understand.

10. Sending and receiving are both enhanced when:

   (a) the parties maintain good eye contact.

   (b) the parties are defensive and challenge one another.

**Answers:** 1(b); 2(a); 3(a); 4(b); 5(b); 6(a); 7(a); 8(a); 9(b); 10(a).

# BUILDING TRUST IN TEAMS

Trust is an essential part of team building. It is important because of the powerful effect it has on every aspect of team performance.

As people work through the team-building processes, they get to know one another. They learn to respect individual differences, appreciate team contributions and enjoy the satisfaction teamwork provides when both personal and organizational goals are achieved.

The following trust statements are actual responses from employees who learned team-building techniques.

"Employees must perceive their managers as open, fair, honest, and willing to listen. Managers must be decisive and stand by their decisions in difficult situations."

"Employees must have the confidence that their manager will support them, even in delicate matters, and take responsibility for group actions. A manager must also readily give credit to employees where credit is due."

"Trust is built in a work group by promoting open communications, providing fair leadership, and supervising with sensitivity."

"Establishing trust in a work group requires open and honest communication, accepting others, sharing a common goal, and respecting the opinions of others on how to achieve that goal."

"Trust is necessary to a productive working environment. This environment of trust promotes loyalty and commitment to achieve the goals and objectives of the organization."

# POSITIVE FEEDBACK LEADS TO TRUST

Trust is impossible in an environment where people are overly criticized or where blaming is common. Fear is not conducive to trust.

Managers can help create a healthy environment through example. Focus on the positive; if criticism must be given, do so in private. Do not blame others for your actions, and do not encourage or reward employees for blaming each other.

Team performance can be improved when all members provide feedback on how well things are being done. Positive recognition when things are done right encourages similar performance in the future. Corrective action to redirect inappropriate or inadequate performance clears the air and can set the stage for future success.

## Praise Is Powerful

There are many forms of recognition, but one of the most powerful is praise. Some managers use praise effectively; others use it poorly or not at all.

Take a moment and review each of your team members, what each does particularly well, and how you could phrase a compliment that is appropriate.

|  | **Job Well Done** | **Praise** |
|---|---|---|
| *Employee A:* | _____ | _____ |
|  | _____ | _____ |
|  | _____ | _____ |
| *Employee B:* | _____ | _____ |
|  | _____ | _____ |
|  | _____ | _____ |

# ASK YOURSELF

► Do you think it is important to help people feel good about themselves?

► Do you give periodic praise to team members for meeting job requirements?

► Do you feel that people respond better to praise of what they do well than to criticism of what they do wrong?

► Do you recognize individual contributions to final results of team effort, not to just the team as a whole?

CHAPTER
NINE

# CONFLICT
# RESOLUTION
# AND
# PROBLEM
# SOLVING

# CONFLICT IS INEVITABLE

Team leaders must accept the fact that any time two or more people are brought together, the stage is set for potential conflict. When conflict does occur, the results may be positive or negative, depending upon how those involved choose to approach it.

With this in mind, team leaders must be sensitive to the fact that positive contributions can arise from conflict—providing things do not get out of control. Teaching team members to understand conflict, and resolve it positively, will help the team succeed.

When team members understand the nature of conflict and constructive methods to resolve it, they can usually work out disagreements themselves. When they can't, or when the problem requires your intervention for other reasons, you may have to engineer a solution.

*Your Turn*

*Ask yourself the following:*

► What types of conflict are most frequent in your organization?

► What is your first reaction to budding conflicts?

► Do you find that you tend to have a set response to conflict?

► Does conflict arouse difficult emotions in yourself or your employees?

► Do you always view conflict as a negative?

# UNDERSTANDING CONFLICT RESOLUTION

There are several basic approaches to problem solving. People adopt one or another out of past experience combined with their own assertiveness level. Positive and negative outcomes can result from both aggressiveness or passiveness if either is extreme. This could perhaps best be explained by this cross-chart:

|  | Positive Outcome | Negative Outcome |
|---|---|---|
| Assertive Disposition | Problem Solving (involves all participants until resolution is achieved) | Win/Lose (one person comes out on top while others lose) |
| Passive Disposition | Cooperative (will give input if others initiate) | Uncooperative (resists arriving at a solution) |

## Behavior and Justification of Conflict-Resolution Styles

Conflict-resolution styles can be changed, but only if each person's style is identified and understood.

Review the chart on page 109 with team members. Discuss ways conflicts can be more effectively resolved in the team and with other units.

# CONFLICT RESOLUTION STYLES

There are five basic approaches to conflict resolution. They can be summarized as follows.

| Style | Characteristic Behavior | User Justification |
|---|---|---|
| **Avoidance** | Non-confrontational. Ignores or passes over issues. Denies issues are a problem. | Differences too minor or too great to resolve. Attempts might damage relationships or create even greater problems. |
| **Accommodating** | Agreeable, non-assertive behavior. Cooperative even at the expense of personal goals. | Not worth risking damage to relationships or general disharmony. |
| **Win/Lose** | Confrontational, assertive and aggressive. Must win at any cost. | Survival of the fittest. Must prove superiority. Most ethically or professionally correct. |
| **Compromising** | Important all parties achieve basic goals and maintain good relationships. Aggressive but cooperative. | No one person or idea is perfect. There is more than one good way to do anything. You must give to get. |
| **Problem Solving** | Needs of both parties are legitimate and important. High respect for mutual support. Assertive and cooperative. | When parties will openly discuss issues, a mutually beneficial solution can be found without anyone making a major concession. |

Conflict becomes unhealthy when it is avoided or approached on a win/lose basis. Animosities will develop, communications will break down, trust and mutual support will deteriorate, and hostilities will result. When sides are chosen productivity will diminish or stop. The damage is usually difficult (sometimes impossible) to repair.

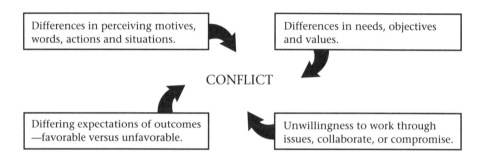

Conflict is healthy when it causes the parties to explore new ideas, test their position and beliefs, and stretch their imagination. When conflict is dealt with constructively, people can be stimulated to greater creativity, which will lead to a wider variety of alternatives and better results.

# MAKE UNDERSTANDING CONFLICT A TEAM PROJECT

Two situations are presented below. In both of these situations everyone means well and, if questioned, would maintain they were trying to accomplish what they perceived to be the best objective. Nonetheless, conflict is present.

Some members of Memorial Church want to use church funds to aid the local poor. Others prefer spending more money for missionary work. Still others think new carpeting for the sanctuary is the greatest need.

A sales manager wants a large inventory of all products so quick deliveries to customers can be promised. The manufacturing manager want to limit the inventory to hold down storage costs.

Conflict is present when there are differences in:

▶ Needs, objectives, and values.

▶ Expectations of outcomes—favorable versus unfavorable.

▶ Unwillingness to work through issues, collaborate, or compromise.

Conflict is healthy when it causes the parties to explore new ideas, test their position and beliefs, and stretch their imagination. When conflict is dealt with constructively, people can be stimulated to greater creativity, which will lead to a wider variety of alternatives and better results.

## Teaching Employees Problem-Solving Techniques

Many owners spend too much time solving problems that could be better handled by the employees they supervise. When owners try to solve all the problems, production is slowed, employees are frustrated, and personal growth is limited. The owner ends up with less time to plan, organize, motivate, and control. Delegation is more effective when the owner participates in problem solving only when necessary, instead of dominating it. In view of this, problem solving should be taught at every level of the organization.

The problem-solving process should be as simple as possible while getting the job done. One basic approach is outlined below. Check those steps that would be useful in your operation:

1. **State what appears to be the problem.**

   The real problem may not surface until facts have been gathered and analyzed. Therefore, start with a supposition that can later be confirmed or corrected.

2. **Gather facts, feelings, and opinions.**

   What happened? Where, when, and how did it occur? What is its size, scope, and severity? Who and what is affected? Is it likely to happen again? Does it need to be corrected? Time and expense may require problem solvers to think through what they need and assign priorities to the more critical elements.

3. **Restate the problem.**

   The facts help make this possible and provide supporting data. The actual problem may or may not be the same as stated in Step 1.

4. **Identify alternative solutions.**

   Generate ideas. Do not eliminate any possible solutions until several have been discussed.

5. **Evaluate alternatives.**

   Which will provide the optimum solution? What are the risks? Are the costs in keeping with the benefits? Will the solution create new problems?

6. **Implement the decision.**

   Who must be involved? To what extent? How, when, and where? Who will the decision impact? What might go wrong? How will results be reported and verified?

7. **Evaluate the results.**

   Test the solution against the desired results. Modify the solution if better results are needed.

# Teaching Employees Self-Control

Discipline is a basic requirement of team performance. A good leader maintains control but strives to establish an environment in which team members will exercise self-control. This is accomplished by following through on the true meaning of discipline, namely, "training that develops or molds by instruction or exercise." The means by which positive discipline can be implemented are listed below.

1. From the outset, make sure team members understand what is expected of them and what standards are to be met.

2. Teach team members how to fulfill expectations and achieve standards.

3. Encourage team members as they make progress toward attaining company goals.

4. Compliment team members when standards are achieved and expectations are realized.

5. Re-direct inadequate or inappropriate performance when it occurs, and repeat 1–4.

6. If the inadequate or inappropriate performance persists after a reasonable period of time (and step 5 has been applied), bench or trade the player. He or she hasn't made the team.

This process, when consistently applied and followed, will eliminate most disciplinary problems. If you have not been doing this, you can institute it immediately with your entire team. Most people want to do the right thing but they often need guidance to know what that is.

*Your Turn*    ***Answer the following true/false questions.***

|  | True | False |
|---|:---:|:---:|
| 1. Teams are more concerned with getting positive results than they are with "turf" considerations. | ☐ | ☐ |
| 2. Trust is a minor factor in most team situations. | ☐ | ☐ |
| 3. Team members need to know anything that affects the work they are performing. | ☐ | ☐ |
| 4. Competition and conflict in a team is healthy if it is properly controlled and quickly resolved. | ☐ | ☐ |
| 5. Open communication in a team will promote understanding, a recognition of individual differences, and encourage mutual support. | ☐ | ☐ |
| 6. Teams participate in decision making but recognize their leader must act on his or her own if a consensus cannot be reached or there is a crisis. | ☐ | ☐ |
| 7. Successful teams have little need for recognition and praise. | ☐ | ☐ |
| 8. Self-control and good discipline are by-products of team building. | ☐ | ☐ |

***Check your answers with the following.***

# Your Turn Answers

1. *True.* Productivity, commitment, open communication, and trust are the usual casualties of "turf" wars.

2. *False.* Trust is one of the most vital ingredients.

3. *True.* The right information makes the job easier.

4. *True.* It is stimulating and mind opening.

5. *True.* Forget this principle at your own risk.

6. *True.* Timeliness is also important in decision making.

7. *False.* Recognition and praise are among the strongest motivators known.

8. *True.* People who are committed to a task, a unit, and each other are not apt to create unnecessary problems.

# ASK YOURSELF

► Is there frequent conflict in your organization? Is it constructive or destructive?

► What are you losing from the bottom line because of current conflicts or grudges held over from poorly resolved or unresolved conflict in the past?

► How do you resolve personal conflict with others in your organization? Are the results win/win?

► What do you do when conflict develops between individuals and/or functional groups within your organization? With customers?

# USING
# DELEGATION
# TO
# IMPROVE
# TEAM
# PERFORMANCE

CHAPTER TEN

## MANAGE-MENT STYLE AND DELE-GATION

Management is a leadership effort to integrate and effectively use a variety of resources to accomplish an objective. It applies to all organizations, whether they are businesses, hospitals, or political entities. Owner/managers will do well to remember there is no one best way to plan, organize, motivate, or control. Each owner must continually increase his or her knowledge of management concepts and draw upon them until a winning combination is found that fits him or her, the people supervised, and the work involved.

One factor is central, however, to every management task. That factor is *delegation*. The owner must define what he/she expects, when it is expected, and how to best employ his or her human resources to obtain the desired results. This means assigning work in a planned and thoughtful way.

Delegation is giving people things to do. Management is accomplishing organizational goals by working through individuals and groups. It is easy to see that the two are closely entwined. And it is obvious that the owner who is not delegating is not managing.

Delegation, of all the skills and activities of an owner, is one of the most indispensable.

*Your Turn*

*Answer the following:*

► Identify the employees in your organization who appear to have free time. Is it due to poor delegation practices? What can you do about it?

► Who are the employees in your organization who do not appear to be working up to their potential? Why not? What can you do about it?

► Ask your employees how challenged they are by their assignments. What changes would increase the challenge and their level of job satisfaction?

# COMMON BARRIERS TO DELEGATION

Ineffective delegators rationalize their inadequacies in various ways. They usually center around obstacles (natural or self-made) in themselves, in the characteristics of their employees, or in the situation itself. In the following list of attitudes, indicate those that affect your delegation practices. Think about each statement carefully and be totally honest.

### Self-Imposed Obstacles

I prefer performing operating tasks—not management functions—because I understand them better and I know how.

I can do the work in my company better than anyone else.

I don't know how to delegate.

My employees won't like me if I expect too much of them.

I am not certain to whom I should delegate.

It is easier and quicker to do things myself.

We just can't afford to make any mistakes.

### Employee-Imposed Obstacles

My employees lack experience and competence.

My employees are already overloaded.

My employees resist responsibility.

My employees fear criticism and avoid risk.

### Situation-Imposed Obstacles

Customers expect me to handle the really important tasks personally.

My employees can't be trusted to work on their own.

We are seriously understaffed. I have no one to whom I can delegate.

Most of our decisions are made under crisis conditions.

If you answered yes to more than a few of the above, you should seriously examine the attitudes that keep you from delegating tasks and responsibilities.

# Symptoms of Poor Delegation

There are many symptoms of poor delegation. They can usually be seen in the work habits of the owner, the attitude of the employees, or the productivity of the group. In the list below, check the symptoms that are visible in your organization.

❏ Deadlines are frequently missed.

❏ Some employees are much busier than others.

❏ The supervisor (me) is usually too busy to talk to employees.

❏ Employees are unsure of their authority.

❏ No one in the unit is ever ready for promotion.

❏ Employee decisions are often overruled.

❏ No one seems to know who is in charge of a project.

❏ The organization is plagued by slow decision making.

❏ The supervisor (me) never has time to visit employee work areas.

❏ Changes in plans and objectives are not passed on to employees with a need to know.

❏ Employees are assigned tasks they can't handle without training.

❏ The supervisor (me) sometimes intervenes in a project or assignment without informing the delegatee.

❏ Employees frequently request transfers to other units.

❏ The communications flow is sporadic, incomplete, and often too late.

❏ The supervisor (me) often takes work home and sometimes reschedules his or her vacation because of the workload.

❏ Talented employees are bored.

❏ The supervisor (me) insists all mail must first pass through his or her office.

If you checked more than one or two of the above statements, you should look carefully at your delegation practices and ask yourself why these conditions exist.

# TECHNICAL, HUMAN, AND CONCEPTUAL SKILLS

Many new supervisors and managers fall into the same trap. They do not see the difference between technical, human, and conceptual skills and how these skills apply to their position. It might help you in delegation if you broke down various responsibilities using these definitions:

### Technical Skills

Ability to use knowledge, methods, and equipment to perform specific task, acquired from experience and training.

### Human Skills

Ability and judgment in working with people, including an understanding of motivation and leadership.

### Conceptual Skills

Ability to understand the complexities of the overall organization and where one's own unit fits into the total picture.

## Level of Skills Required

Lower-level supervisors need considerable technical skill because they are often required to train and develop new employees and technicians. At the other extreme, senior managers do not need to know how to perform all the specific tasks at the operational level, but they should understand how all the functions are interrelated. The common denominator that is crucial at all levels is human skill.

As supervisors move up in management, they must learn to delegate jobs requiring technical skill to their subordinates, to give themselves time to learn the human and conceptual skills now required of them.

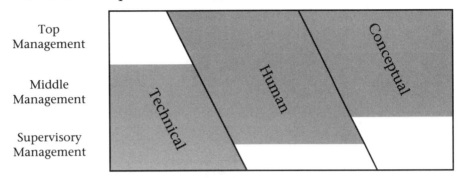

After viewing this chart, can you think of some functions you are more willing to delegate?

## Delegating Versus Doing

Some managers have trouble sharing responsibility, while others simply enjoy the technical tasks upon which they founded their business.

However, a manager who expects to expand his or her business will be doing more and more delegating, versus "doing" the original task him or herself. The shift in proportion of tasks is illustrated in this chart.

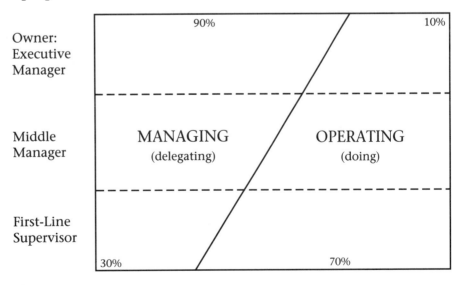

# CASE STUDY

## The Do-It-Yourself Owner

Joanne was a capable and enthusiastic professional. Her success in a corporate environment as a professional practitioner led her to believe she could start her own business and manage five professionals doing work very similar to what she had personally performed in the past.

She began her new business thinking, "I was more successful than others in the past. Therefore, my expertise is probably greater than that of any of the people I have just hired, and I can do most of the work better and faster than they can. I will train them when I have time, but right now I had better concentrate on getting the work out."

Joanne did not pass on any major assignments to her employees—she did the work herself. As time passed, her hours of work increased steadily and she was less and less available to her customers. Her employees were given only the most routine work, receiving no training, and actually knew very little about major projects in progress. One actually resigned because of the lack of challenge and personal growth. Joanne was too busy to replace him.

Finally, after sixty days, Joanne went to her old supervisor where she used to work for advice.

What would you have told Joanne if you had been her former supervisor? Please summarize your comments below.

_____

_____

_____

## Response to Case Study

Joanne's former supervisor didn't waste time getting to the point. She simply asked her to talk about her workload and that of her subordinates. The contrast made the problem obvious. When Joanne explained her rationale, the supervisor would not buy it. She suggested Joanne take a good look at her subordinates and their past work record. Most were high achievers when given the chance. She suggested that Joanne was afraid to let go of responsibility and authority and perhaps enjoyed "doing" work more than "managing" work. Joanne then admitted that perhaps she didn't know how to let go and still maintain control. The discussion concluded with Joanne agreeing to attend a seminar on delegating.

# SIX LEVELS OF AUTHORITY

A common management mistake is failing to delegate the right amount of authority considering the task, the surrounding circumstances, and the employee's ability. Some managers do not delegate any authority because they want full personal control. Others give full authority because they want to be free of the task. Most of the time, something in between these two extremes is called for. Before you make your next delegation, review the authority levels described here and select one that fits your needs.

| Level of Authority | Reason |
|---|---|
| 1. "Look into the situation. Get all the facts and report them to me. I'll decide what to do." | The employee is new to the job and the supervisor wants to retain control of the outcome. |
| 2. "Identify the problem. Determine alternative solutions and the pluses and minuses of each. Recommend one for my approval." | The employee is being developed and the supervisor wants to see how he or she approaches problems and makes decisions. |
| 3. "Examine the issues. Let me know what you intend to do, but don't take action until you check with me." | The supervisor has confidence in the employee, but does not want action taken without his or her approval. This may be because of constraints from higher management or the need to communicate the action to others before it is taken. |
| 4. "Solve the problem. Let me know what you intend to do, then do it, unless I say 'no'." | The supervisor has respect for the employee's ability and judgment and only wants a final check before action is taken. |
| 5. "Take action on this matter, and let me know what you did." | The supervisor has full confidence in the employee and has no need to be consulted before action is taken. He or she wants to know the outcome. |
| 6. "Take action. No further contact with me is necessary." | The supervisor has total confidence in the employee. The employee has full authority to act and does not need to report the results back to the supervisor. |

# WHAT CAN DELEGATING DO FOR ME?

New owner/managers often assign a low priority to delegation because they are unsure of how to go about it and don't see the benefits. Some actually think delegation is more trouble than it's worth. Some *advantages of good delegation* are listed on the following page.

1. More work can be accomplished and deadlines can be met more easily.

2. Employees become involved and committed.

3. The assignment of specific responsibility and authority makes control less difficult.

4. Employees grow and develop.

5. Human resources are utilized more fully and productivity improves.

6. Individual performance can be measured more accurately.

7. Compensation, including merit increases, can be more directly related to individual performance.

8. A diversity of products, operations, and people can be managed effectively.

9. Distant operations can be managed with less travel and stress.

10. Employee satisfaction and recognition are enhanced.

11. The owner has time for planning, organizing, motivating, and controlling.

12. The owner is freed to do those tasks only he or she can do.

Please add any other advantages you can think of in the spaces below.

13. _____

14. _____

15. _____

# FACT VERSUS FANCY

The attitudes that prevent you from delegating need to be examined objectively. They usually are invalid and keep supervisors from delegating as they should. Several of them deserve close scrutiny.

## The Fallacy of Omnipotence

This is the "I can do it better myself" syndrome. Even if it is true, the choice is not between the quality of the supervisor's work on a given task and that of the employee. The choice is between the benefits of the supervisor's performance on a single task versus the benefits of spending his or her time in planning, organizing, motivating, controlling, and developing an effective team. The team will eventually outperform the manager and continue to grow.

## The Fear of Being Disliked

Though few managers will admit it, most are concerned that their employees will dislike or resent them if they press them with a lot of work. Such a manager will risk personal burnout rather than inconvenience an employee.

Interestingly enough, employees rate supervisors who make full use of delegation "good" or "excellent." Poor delegators receive low ratings.

## Lack of Confidence in Employees

Owners who lack confidence in their employees should look to themselves for the answer. They are, or should be, in control of the situation.

If employees cannot handle delegated assignments, the owner/manager has either hired incompetent people, failed to provide them with appropriate training, or has not made the effort to find out the extent of their capabilities. The remedy: identify strengths and weaknesses and train or replace those who still cannot meet standards.

### Employees Expect the Answers from Me

This is usually how managers rationalize taking problem solving and decision making away from employees. It occurs when an employee brings a problem to a supervisor who says, "Why don't you leave it with me and I'll get back to you." When the supervisor does get back to the employee it is with the solution. The employee only wanted to talk about the problem—she didn't want the answer.

### I Can Do It Faster Than I Can Explain It

A supervisor who uses this excuse to justify doing an operating task that he or she likes to do, but someone else could be taught to do, is making a serious mistake. If he or she doesn't take the time to teach someone else the task, he or she will still be performing it far into the future. This consumes valuable time and effort that could be better spent on tasks only the supervisor can do.

## How Well Do You Delegate?

Here is an opportunity to learn how well you delegate. This scale will help identify your strengths and determine where improvement would be beneficial. Circle the number that best describes you. The higher the number, the more the statement describes you. When you have finished, total the numbers circled in the space provided.

1. Each of my employees knows what I expect of her or him.                     7 6 5 4 3 2 1

2. I involve employees in goal setting, problem solving, and productivity-improvement activities.                     7 6 5 4 3 2 1

3. I place my personal emphasis on planning, organizing, motivating, and controlling, rather than doing tasks others could do.                     7 6 5 4 3 2 1

4. When assigning work, I select the assignee thoughtfully.                     7 6 5 4 3 2 1

5. When a problem occurs on a project I have delegated, I give the employee a reasonable chance to work it out for him/herself.

7 6 5 4 3 2 1

6. When I delegate work to employees, I brief them fully on the details with which I am familiar.

7 6 5 4 3 2 1

7. I see delegation as one way to help employees develop their skills, and I assign work accordingly.

7 6 5 4 3 2 1

8. I support and help employees in emergencies, but I do not permit them to leave work for me to do.

7 6 5 4 3 2 1

9. When I assign work, I stress the results desired, not how to accomplish them.

7 6 5 4 3 2 1

10. When I delegate a project, I make sure everyone concerned knows who is in charge.

7 6 5 4 3 2 1

11. When delegating work, I balance authority with need and experience.

7 6 5 4 3 2 1

12. I hold my employees responsible for results.

7 6 5 4 3 2 1

TOTAL _____

A score between 72 and 84 suggests you are on target. A score between 48 and 71 indicates you are getting by, but could improve. Anything below 48 means you need to make changes.

# ASK YOURSELF

▶ What specific symptoms of poor delegation do you see in your organization? What will you do about them?

▶ Who is the best delegator in your organization? Can he/she coach others in the process?

▶ Is it possible your delegation practices inhibit delegation by others within your organization?

▶ How much would improved efficiency in the work flow add to your bottom line?

# CHOOSING

# WHAT

# TO

# DELEGATE

## THE FIRST STEP: ANALYZE YOUR JOB AS OWNER

To become an effective delegator, you must have your own job well in hand. This means periodically:

▶ Reviewing your duties and responsibilities as an owner of a business. How have they changed over time? How do they affect your company? What are the new challenges? What old practices need to be stopped?

▶ Reaffirming the primary objectives of your company. Have there been any changes that affect priorities or that need to be communicated to employees?

▶ Highlighting key result areas. What are the make or break factors in your role as owner? What are the areas in which specific results are essential?

▶ Reexamining your workload to identify those few tasks only you can do.

Remember, you are a manager, not an individual contributor. It is your job to utilize your human resources effectively to accomplish organizational goals. You must sort out the important from the unimportant and proceed on a priority basis. The more you develop your people, and the more you delegate to them, the more they can help you identify key result areas and meet objectives. Let go of tasks that rightfully belong to your employees. That includes troubleshooting and problem solving in their areas of responsibility. Be sure they are properly trained and help them when they flounder, but by all means give them a chance to do the job for which they were hired.

## DECIDING WHAT TO DELEGATE

Any time you perform a task someone else could do, you keep yourself from a task only you can do!

Managers usually delegate to give themselves more time to do complex and difficult management tasks, to improve productivity, or to develop their employees. Some types of work you should consider delegating are listed on the following pages.

## Decisions You Make Most Frequently

Minor decisions and repetitive routines often consume a major portion of the day. Most, if not all, of these can be delegated by teaching employees the policies and procedures that apply. They probably already know the details better than you.

List two possibilities:

1. _____

2. _____

## Functions That Are in Your Technical or Functional Specialty

These are usually operating tasks rather than management functions. You can teach others to do them. In fact, your challenge as a manager is to motivate others to produce better results than you ever did as an individual performer. Part of the time you save can be used to learn about other functions you supervise, so you can manage them better.

List two possibilities:

1. _____

2. _____

## Tasks and Projects for Which You Are Least Qualified

It is almost certain that some of your employees are better qualified and can do parts of the job better than you. Let them.

List two possibilities:

1. _____

2. _____

## Functions You Dislike

Performing functions we dislike is distasteful, and we often put them off or do them poorly. Examine the likes and dislikes of your staff as well as their talents. You will nearly always find someone who likes the job and can do it well. If he or she needs training, provide it.

List two possibilities:

1. _____

2. _____

## Work That Will Provide Experience for Employees

This makes growth in the present job a reality and helps keep employees challenged and motivated.

List two possibilities:

1. _____

2. _____

## Assignments That Will Add Variety to Routine Work

A change of pace is usually welcome and is often a good motivator for an employee whose job is growing dull.

List two possibilities:

1. _____

2. _____

## Activities That Will Make a Position More Complete

As employees become more proficient, they often have time to spare. Add complementary duties and responsibilities to give their positions more substance.

List two possibilities:

1. _____

2. _____

### Tasks That Will Increase the Number of People Who Can Perform Critical Assignments

Maximize the strength of the group by giving people the needed experience to back one another up during emergencies or periods of unusually heavy work.

List two possibilities:

1. _____

2. _____

### Opportunities to Use and Reinforce Creative Talents

Employees are not creative in a stifling environment. Stimulate them with difficult problems and projects and reward creative solutions.

List two possibilities:

1. _____

2. _____

# DIFFERENCES BETWEEN DELEGATORS

The owner's attitude toward employees and their ability to handle delegated assignments can make a significant difference. The successful delegator is characterized by these traits:

► Concentrates on successful results and high goals.

► Reinforces employees' strengths and abilities. Confident of success.

► Encourages employee participation in setting goals and objectives.

► Readily accepts new ideas and creative solutions.

► Communicates freely and openly. Nothing is held back.

► Recognizes achievement and reinforces it.

► Looks at the implications of each assignment for the future and assigns tasks accordingly.

► Encourages employees to appraise their performance and suggest improvements.

### Targeting Areas of Delegation

The following illustration summarizes what you have learned so far and may help you identify areas you can delegate.

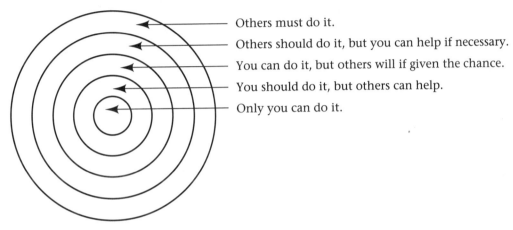

Others must do it.

Others should do it, but you can help if necessary.

You can do it, but others will if given the chance.

You should do it, but others can help.

Only you can do it.

Targeted Delegation

# PLANNING TO DELEGATE

Deciding *what* to delegate is only the first step in the delegation process. Delegation, like other management tasks, is most successful when it's planned. It may take a few minutes, for simple tasks; or a few hours, when the project is complex. Your planning should include the following considerations. Fill out a checklist like this for every major area you are considering delegating.

1. What is the task and objective to be accomplished?

   _____

2. What are the critical completion dates?

   _____

3. What standards will have to be met?

_____

4. What decisions will have to be made?

_____

5. How much authority *can* I delegate?

_____

6. How much authority *will* I delegate?

_____

7. What instructions or orders will the person(s) be authorized to issue?

_____

8. Does a budget need to be developed or followed?

_____

9. Who will the person(s) need to interface with in my unit? In other units?

_____

10. What information do I need to give?

_____

11. How much do I want to be involved?

_____

12. What feedback do I want and when do I want it?

_____

13. Who will I need to keep informed of progress?

_____

**14.** Do I need to tell others who is in charge?

_____

**15.** To whom should I delegate?

_____

---

*Your Turn*    *Complete the following activity.*

➤ Make a list of tasks that only you can do.

➤ After each item you listed, explain why you cannot delegate it. Double-check your reasons to find at least one item you can delegate.

---

# CASE STUDY

## The Delegation Disaster

When Jim bought System Dynamics, Inc., he made up his mind to change the environment and hopefully the attitudes of the employees. The previous owner had not been an effective delegator or communicator. The employees had little to do in a company where the owner was completely swamped.

Jim immediately began to delegate assignments (at fairly high authority levels) that the previous owner had performed herself. He was surprised at the results.

His employees seemed to think he was pushing *his* work on them. Most of them complained they were neither trained nor paid to do the assignments delegated. It was not unusual for them to bring problems arising from their normal assignments to Jim for solutions, and they did not understand him saying, "Don't bring me problems, bring me solutions."

Has Jim overlooked anything in his approach to turning this situation around? Make your comments in the space below.

_____

_____

_____

_____

_____

_____

## Response to Case Study

Jim is to be commended for realizing the need to delegate, but he moved too quickly and without preparing the people properly.

Jim should have taken the time to get to know each person and to learn something about his or her needs, abilities, and goals. It would also have been helpful to share his management style and personal goals for the organization. A gradual increase in delegated tasks with employees participating in determining the authority level would have been less threatening to the employees, since they did not seem to understand delegation or have confidence in their ability to undertake new assignments.

*Your Turn*    *Answer the following.*

➤ Describe some of your delegation disasters. What went wrong?

➤ List some incidents where your failure to delegate delayed action on a critical issue or caused you an excessive amount of work and worry.

➤ Review an incident where you delegated a difficult task reluctantly and it was completed by the delegatee with outstanding results.

## Test Yourself

Answer the following true/false questions.

|  |  | True | False |
|---|---|:---:|:---:|
| 1. | Most owners excel at delegation. | ☐ | ☐ |
| 2. | Delegation is an indispensable management skill. | ☐ | ☐ |
| 3. | Delegation is essential to the development of employees and the improvement of productivity. | ☐ | ☐ |
| 4. | Employees dislike managers who delegate. | ☐ | ☐ |
| 5. | Delegation is one way to use and reinforce creative talents. | ☐ | ☐ |
| 6. | Managers must always keep key result areas in mind when delegating. | ☐ | ☐ |
| 7. | Delegation is a positive act and requires very little thought or preparation. | ☐ | ☐ |
| 8. | You don't really know what people can do until you give them a chance under the proper conditions. | ☐ | ☐ |
| 9. | The goal in delegation is the satisfactory completion of the assigned task through the personal efforts of those assigned the task. | ☐ | ☐ |
| 10. | Teaching employees to solve problems helps prepare them for delegation. | ☐ | ☐ |

Check your answers with those on the following page.

## Test Yourself Answers

1. *False.* Name five in your circle of acquaintances.

2. *True.* If you are not delegating, you are not managing.

3. *True.* Try it; you'll like the results.

4. *False.* Research reflects just the opposite.

5. *True.* If you don't delegate, creativity will die.

6. *True.* Accomplishing results in key results areas is what you job is all about.

7. *False.* Thought and preparation assure success.

8. *True.* Everyone needs a chance to show what they can do.

9. *True.* Too much interference spoils the results.

10. *True.* It will make your life much easier.

# DEVELOPING A PERSONAL ACTION PLAN

Think over the material you have read. Review the self-analysis questionnaire and the case study. What have you learned about delegation? What have you learned about yourself as a delegator? How can you apply what you have learned? Make a commitment to yourself to become a better delegator and a more effective manager by designing a personal action plan to help you accomplish this goal.

The following guide may help you clarify your goals and outline the actions required to achieve them.

1. My current delegation skills are effective in the following areas:

   _____

   _____

2. I need to improve my delegation skills in the following areas:

_____

_____

3. My goals for improving my delegation skills are as follows (be sure they are specific, attainable, and measurable):

_____

_____

4. Following are my action steps, along with a timetable, to accomplish each goal:

_____

_____

# ASK YOURSELF

► Are you doing a cursory job of preparation when delegating?

► Do you have a delegation plan or do you just dump assignments on whoever is around?

► What three specific things will you do in the future to make your delegation more effective?

# SELECTING
# THE
# RIGHT
# PERSON
# FOR
# DELEGATION

## SELECTING THE RIGHT PERSON

As soon as you have completed your delegation plan, identify the appropriate person to perform the task. Some of the many things to consider are listed below.

### Does the Work Belong to a Particular Position?

Some tasks or projects fit right into existing work assignments and can be logically delegated there.

List two examples from the past or two possibilities for the future:

1. _____

2. _____

### Who Has the Interest and/or the Ability?

Analyze employee job performance periodically, and keep an inventory of the interests and abilities of your staff. Look for opportunities to give employees who are attending classes a chance to apply what they are learning.

Give consideration to interest as well as ability. A minimally qualified person may take the assignment enthusiastically and develop the required skills; the best-qualified person with a low level of interest may do a poor job.

List two examples from the past or two prospects for the future:

1. _____

2. _____

### Who Will Find the Work Challenging?

Studies reflect that large numbers of employees are unchallenged, and their boredom is reflected in their performance. Give them the pleasure of a new opportunity to achieve.

List two prospects for the future:

1. _____

2. _____

### Who Will the Assignment Stretch and Help to Grow?

Some employees thrive on challenge and are willing to develop new skills to meet new job requirements. Give them the opportunity.

Identify two people in this category:

1. _____

2. _____

### Who Has Been Overlooked When You Have Delegated in the Past?

Delegate to all of your employees and stretch them when you can. Avoid playing favorites or overburdening some of your staff.

Delegating to an employee who has been untested in the past requires careful planning, but the payoff in added performance is potentially high.

An assignment delegated with care can bring a problem employee up to standard. An employee with unused potential can be motivated to new heights of achievement.

Every time you give an "unknown" the chance to perform in a new way, the overall depth, versatility, and morale of your unit will improve.

List two possibilities for the future:

1. _____

2. _____

### Who Has the Time?

If an employee has occasional periods with a light workload, look for opportunities to productively use that employee's time.

List two possibilities:

1. _____

2. _____

### Who Is Being Prepared for a New Assignment or Promotion?

Employees being prepared for a new assignment or promotion often profit from delegated assignments that relate to their new duties and responsibilities.

List two possibilities:

1. _____

2. _____

# REMEMBERING YOUR SECRETARY'S POTENTIAL

Managers with secretaries or administrative assistants often fail to delegate properly to them. They see them only as someone to do word processing, answer the telephones, and keep up the files. This is a major mistake.

When secretaries have been properly trained and participate actively in the management of their supervisor's business affairs, they can be of incalculable value in a number of areas. Consider the following possibilities. As you do, be alert to the tasks you already delegate to your secretary or administrative assistant as well as new ways to enrich their jobs and facilitate your own:

1. Screening and directing mail to the proper person for action.

2. Composing correspondence for your signature.

3. Organizing your time, coordinating appointments, and assuring deadlines are met.

4. Following up on reports and other work on which you, or others, have set a due date, and reporting their status to you.

5. Coordinating conference calls.

6. Organizing and setting up meetings on your behalf.

7. Gathering information needed for decision making.

8. Maintaining appropriate personal records and files.

9. Redirecting telephone calls and correspondence that come to you, but should go elsewhere.

10. Performing basic research on projects you have retained for yourself.

11. Maintaining confidential records.

12. Facilitating communication through your office in your absence.

Add other possibilities that fit your situation:

_____

_____

_____

# MAKING THE PREDELEGATION ASSESSMENT

The planning phase prior to assigning work is the owner's opportunity to organize the distribution of work and to schedule it properly. The quality of your preparations will largely determine the success of the delegation. Owners who ignore the planning are usually those who are keeping far too much work for themselves or those who indiscriminately dump assignments on staff members. Asking yourself the following questions in advance will help you make better delegation decisions:

1. What work needs to be done?

_____

2. What can and should be delegated?

_____

3. What is the best match of work with individual employee abilities and interests?

_____

4. Who would the assignment help develop?

_____

5. Who can do it for me now?

_____

6. Who can be trained to do it?

_____

7. What is the employee's current workload and level of performance?

_____

8. What is my best course of action, other than doing it myself, given the time constraints involved?

_____

# COMMUNICATING THE DELEGATION

The heart of the delegation process is the interaction between the supervisor and the employee when the assignment is made.

This face-to-face, two-way discussion is the critical step that should end with employee commitment and the supervisor's assurance that the results needed will be achieved.

Delegation is not just pushing work down. When you are delegating, you are consulting and developing as well as assigning work. Open communication is vital, and success depends ultimately on the communication skills of the manager and the employee and on the quality of their relationship. When there is a lack of trust on either side, or poor communication between them, the needed understanding and motivation is unlikely to be there.

The following steps are essential in communicating an assignment:

1. **Describe as fully as possible the project or task and the results expected.**

   Pass on all the information needed to get the job started, or let the employee know where it can be obtained. Indicate who else will be involved and describe their roles.

2. **Agree on standards of performance and timetables.**

   The scope of the assignment has already been determined, but you will want the employee's input on standards and a reasonable timetable for completion of the assignment.

3. **Determine any training or special help that will be needed, and when it will be provided.**

4. **Define parameters and the resources, including budget, that will be available.**

5. **State the amount and frequency of feedback you expect.**

6. **Spell out the amount of authority being delegated.**

   This should be balanced according to the complexity of the task, your confidence in the employee, and your need to keep others informed.

7. **Tell others who is in charge.**

   It is important you do not become a communications block between the delegatee and others who will be involved or affected.

It is easy to see from these seven basic points that delegation is *not* more trouble than it's worth. Have you been missing some good opportunities because you thought it was?

# MISSED OPPORTUNITIES

Owners who find themselves deeply involved in the detailed work of their business sometimes wake up to the fact that the business is controlling them—they are controlling nothing. If they examine the situation carefully (while pondering the fact that their employees went home hours ago and they are still working), they often see the reason for their plight. Their reaction is usually, "If I had delegated this to Clifford or Sue in the first place, I wouldn't be having this problem now."

How many times have you missed the opportunity to delegate, or thought you had, and found yourself doing work someone else could and should have done?

By now, some missed opportunities to delegate have no doubt come to mind. List them in the space provided below . . . and resolve not to let it happen again.

_____

_____

_____

_____

_____

_____

*Your Turn*

*Answer the following:*

► Have you considered everyone in the organization in your delegation plan?

► What steps will you take to make all employees aware of the benefits of sound delegation practices?

# FOLLOWING THROUGH

The goal in delegation is satisfactory completion of the assigned task or project through the personal efforts of those handling tasks.

It is important, however, that the manager follow through with any support, resources, or information promised. It is also important that a feedback mechanism, suitable to the situation, be established between the employee assigned and the manager. These considerations are all part of the preparations for delegation, and should be covered when the delegation is made. The essential elements of follow through are presented here.

Your goals are to:

► Encourage independence. Allow freedom of action in keeping with the level of delegation. Support initiative and creativity.

► To share opinions and show interest.

► Teach the employee to accept mistakes and learn from them.

► Provide counsel or training when needed.

In order to accomplish this, you must:

► Be available.

► Don't take the job back unless absolutely essential (coach through problems).

► Share all pertinent information.

► Monitor progress, but do not hover.

► Provide honest feedback.

► Suggest corrections if appropriate.

► Help solve problems, but only those beyond the employee's ability to handle.

► Evaluate performance. Plan any needed training for the future.

► Compliment efforts and reward success.

# CASE STUDY

## Making Choices

Susan has been managing her own business for approximately two years. Previously she had been a very effective individual performer in a major corporation. She has had limited supervisory experience. Delegation is very difficult for her, but she is making a real effort to learn to do it well. She has eight employees.

An associate asked her recently how she was doing with her delegation efforts. Susan replied, "I think I am doing pretty well. I have learned that Mary Wong is very knowledgeable about all aspects of the work, and she always completes the assignments I give her on time—even if she has to work overtime and on the weekends. So I give her all the big jobs and let the others stick to the routines they know best. My other employees just aren't qualified to carry the burden that Mary does."

If you were Susan's associate, how would you respond?

_____

_____

_____

_____

_____

_____

# Response to Case Study

It is good that Susan has identified Mary Wong's strengths and is delegating to her. However, she may be delegating so much that Mary is carrying an unfair share of the load and other employees are being prevented from learning new things. Balancing tasks between employees is always difficult, especially when there are one or two you know can do it all and the others would be a risk.

You can minimize the risk when assigning work to employees you don't know well by planning the delegation carefully, following up on progress frequently, and training as necessary. Otherwise, you and your "Mary Wongs" will be doing all the important and complex work yourselves and your other employees will be stagnating.

# A Delegation Checklist

The following checklist is designed to guide the owner through the delegation process.

1. **Personal Preparation**

   I have reviewed my job and analyzed or identified:

   ❏ My duties and responsibilities

   ❏ Key results areas

   ❏ Objectives

   ❏ Management tasks versus operating work

   ❏ The assignments I can delegate

2. **Planning the Delegation**

   I have planned the delegation and established or considered:

   ❏ The objectives to be accomplished

   ❏ Completion dates

   ❏ Standards to be met

❑ The decision making required

❑ The amount of authority to be delegated

❑ Budget and other resource requirements

❑ How involved I want to be

❑ What feedback I want and when I want it

❑ The person to whom I will delegate

3. **Selecting the Right Person**

I have selected an employee after considering:

❑ To whom the work logically belongs

❑ Who has the interest or the ability

❑ Who will find the work challenging

❑ Who the assignment will help develop

❑ Who has been overlooked in the past

❑ Who is best qualified

❑ Who has the time

❑ Who will do the best job

4. **Making the Delegation**

When I communicate the delegation I will:

❑ Describe the task and results expected

❑ Agree on standards of performance and timetables

❑ Determine training needs and when training will be provided

❑ State the amount and frequency of feedback I expect

❑ Define parameters and resources, including budgets

❑ Spell out the level of authority

❑ Tell others who is in charge

### 5. Following Through

I will follow through by:

- ❏ Setting reasonable reporting and review schedules

- ❏ Respecting the level of delegation given

- ❏ Communicating freely and openly

- ❏ Supporting the employee to the extent required

- ❏ Offering encouragement and reinforcing employee strengths and abilities

- ❏ Recognizing achievement

- ❏ Intervening only if *absolutely* necessary

## What You Should Expect

The owner has every right to expect results from the employee according to the parameters established when the delegation was made. If these expectations are to be met, the employee must be prepared in advance, permitted to grow as the work is done, and continuously developed for heavier assignments in the future.

The following items can also serve as a checklist for you. If you are successfully delegating, these statements should be true.

1. The employee has a willing, can-do attitude and accepts responsibility for the task.

2. The employee asks questions and seeks help when needed.

3. Progress reports are furnished on time to you and to others in the communications loop.

4. The finished tasks are good examples of completed staff work.

5. The employee uses initiative and shows dedication and commitment to the task.

6. Time, money, equipment, and manpower are seen as expensive resources and used accordingly.

# DELEGATOR'S TROUBLESHOOTING GUIDE

| Possible Problems | Possible Solutions |
|---|---|
| 1. Only meaningless chores are delegated. | Delegating only meaningless chores creates resentment. Mix in some of your favorite things and share the good times. |
| 2. Employees resist the work, claiming they don't know how to do it. | Provide training as necessary, or break down the job and let them handle as many components as they can. Add more as they learn. |
| 3. The employee says he or she is too busy. | If that is true, consider giving the task to someone else, but verify their workload first. |
| 4. The task is repetitive, but it would take you longer to delegate the job than to do it yourself. | Get smart. At least have someone start to learn the process. Soon he or she will be doing it all. Otherwise, you will still be doing it next year. |
| 5. "My customers expect me to sign invoices and other basic documents." | Let your customers know that employees responsible for their account sign as a part of quality control. |
| 6. "Poor results on this project might cost us a customer." | Your job is to let subordinates develop by taking on new endeavors. They may make some mistakes, but they will learn from them. You can minimize serious mistakes by using an appropriate level of delegation. |
| 7. "If my employees can do the tough jobs well, I'm not needed." | You are still needed. Use the free time it gives you to build the business. |
| 8. "My customer expects me to do this personally." | If that is the actual case, you had better do it, but first check it out with the customer. She/he may just want to be sure you see that it gets done. |

| Possible Problems | Possible Solutions |
|---|---|
| 9. "I'll lose my skills if I delegate too much of the work." | Owners need to learn to manage. They need to teach their employees the skills needed for what they used to do. |
| 10. "If I delegate all my work, I won't have anything to do." | Direct your attention to planning, organizing, motivating, and controlling. |
| 11. "I don't understand the work well enough to control it or make a judgment about how well it is being done." | Learn enough about unfamiliar areas to ask the right questions and assess the answers. |
| 12. Employees with delegated tasks keep coming back for advice and help. | Whenever an employee asks how you would do the task, turn it around and ask how she or he would do it. Reinforce correct answers warmly. If you feel sure she or he can handle the problem, or the consequences of an error are low, be unavailable. Help them build confidence. |
| 13. Some employees are overburdened and others don't have enough to do. | The owner is overdelegating to those who are most trusted, and failing to develop those in whom she or he lacks confidence. It is essential to balance the work and raise the confidence level by giving everyone a chance to perform. |
| 14. Employees do not understand organizational objectives and standards. | Tell the employees what is at stake and the *why* of the job. As often as you can, involve the employees in setting objectives and standards. |
| 15. "Employees don't do things the way I do." | Concentrate on getting the right results and learn to live with differences. You may even learn something new. |

| Possible Problems | Possible Solutions |
|---|---|
| 16. The owner either delegates everything or nothing. | Do not give *responsibility* without some *authority* to carry out the mission. |
| 17. The owner assigns the least challenging work to the most qualified people. | Sometimes necessary, but often done because the supervisor fears mistakes. Select a level of delegation that fits the employee and the situation. Some mistakes will occur; they will provide learning experiences. It's a serious mistake to burn out your best people. |
| 18. The owner and the employee have trouble agreeing on the specifics of the delegation. | Review and clarify objectives, to be sure they are understood. Delegate accordingly. Don't be a nitpicker. Follow up as necessary to see that the right results are being obtained. |
| 19. The employee's performance is jeopardizing a successful outcome. | Identify the reason and take corrective action. This might include changing the level of authority and providing more support. Acting carelessly could shatter the employee's confidence. |
| 20. Deadlines are not being met. | Reassess objectives, standards, and priorities with the employee. Identify the reasons for missed deadlines. |

# ASK YOURSELF

► How effectively are you teaching others to do those operating tasks at which you excel?

► Are you making a genuine effort to learn management skills and put them to use?

► Who are the people in your company that are making the transition from being excellent personal practitioners to team leaders? Are they getting the training they need to do this effectively?

► Do you have any team leaders who would be more effective team members?

# CHAPTER THIRTEEN

# COACHING: THE ROLE OF TEAM LEADER

# IDENTIFY-ING THE COACHES IN YOUR LIFE

Forming a team, developing the personal skills of its members, and enabling them to work together effectively are only the initial steps in team building. These first steps must be sustained by continuous analysis of results and corresponding adjustments in member contributions and the game plan to meet changing objectives. The team leader, therefore, must be an adept coach who is constantly improving and applying coaching techniques to meet the needs of the situation and the team.

Most managers can identify people who have influenced their lives in some particular way. The people involved may include parents, friends, teachers, associates or supervisors. In some instances, this influence has been profound, perhaps even changing the course of their lives.

Think about it and make some notes in the space provided.

Who influenced you?

_____

_____

In what way were you influenced?

_____

_____

_____

Would you be who you are today without those influences?

Yes ☐        No ☐

Who influences you now?

_____

_____

Who do you influence?

_____

_____

What outcomes do you have the power to influence?

_____

_____

# WHY COACHING IS IMPORTANT

Few people who achieve a position of leadership can truly claim sole responsibility for their accomplishment. Someone helped them. Someone who knew the goals of the organization and the individual, and who was willing to devote some effort to the satisfaction of both.

This action may have been so subtle, so natural, so well organized, or so well woven into the fabric of the relationship, that it is visible only in retrospect. Owners who have this kind of positive impact on their employees recognize the helping relationship is fundamental to the development of a strong organization.

In this role of helping people grow and adjust to change, the owner is a coach. He or she provides guidance and support but realizes the employee must also help him/herself.

The owner must not only realize helping is a basic function of supervision, but must also let team members know that he or she is available and wants to help them. Sometimes this help comes in the form of reassurance and empathy. Sometimes it just involves listening and reflecting. But more importantly, coaching means giving people challenges, delegating responsibilities, giving them opportunities to get involved, and to grow and develop by learning from their own successes and their own mistakes.

Owners who are committed to coaching see this function not as a luxury to be carried out when time permits, but as an absolute necessity. They have experienced the results that occur when employees are encouraged to work at their potential. They have enjoyed the increased productivity and appreciated the strengthening of their organization as individuals begin to demonstrate their competence and improve their contribution to the team.

## Rate Your Skills as a Coach

Rate your coaching effectiveness on the following rating scale. A five indicates you consider yourself outstanding; a four, very good; a three, satisfactory; a two, needs improvement; a one, poor. To check your ratings, ask your employees to rate you on the same scale.

1. I recognize differences in my staff and coach them accordingly.   5 4 3 2 1

2. I keep my employees informed about organizational plans and operating systems.   5 4 3 2 1

3. I encourage employee suggestions on the implementation of change.   5 4 3 2 1

4. I encourage employees to solve their own problems.   5 4 3 2 1

5. I make sure each employee has a continuing understanding of what is expected of him/her.   5 4 3 2 1

6. I level with employees about their performance.   5 4 3 2 1

7. I help employees prepare for the future.   5 4 3 2 1

8. I give praise and other appropriate rewards to recognize achievement.   5 4 3 2 1

9. I keep employees focused on team effectiveness but keep everyone aware of the value of their personal contributions.   5 4 3 2 1

10. I "bench" employees who fail consistently as team players and who do not respond to coaching.                    5 4 3 2 1

11. I know the personal aspirations of each member of my team.                    5 4 3 2 1

12. I look for ways to help people grow on the job.    5 4 3 2 1

13. I ask other team members to assist one another to learn and to grow.    5 4 3 2 1

14. I make sure team members understand the success of our team and each of its members (myself included) depends on them.                    5 4 3 2 1

15. I make myself available to the team and to individuals on a high-priority basis.                    5 4 3 2 1

16. I do not discourage conflict but I insist it be resolved in a timely manner.                    5 4 3 2 1

17. I work hard to assure team members understand, respect, and support one another.                    5 4 3 2 1

18. I share my knowledge and expertise with the team and expect the same in return.                    5 4 3 2 1

If you scored less than four on any item, that practice should become a target for personal improvement.

## The Coaching Process

The owner who wants to improve coaching skills can start by focusing on what an employee needs to survive and to support self-development. Here are some of these needs along with some coaching methods that will provide appropriate help. Use them as a checklist to measure how well you are doing and as a guide for growth.

| What Employees Need to Develop | Coaching Methods to Help |
|---|---|
| 1. A basic understanding of his/her job and its contribution to the team. | An owner enables this by:<br><br>• Developing with the employee what the job is, particularly basic functions and relationships.<br>• Involving the employee in goal setting.<br>• Jointly establishing standards for accuracy, punctuality, efficiency, etc. |
| 2. A continuing understanding of what is expected from him or her. | An owner facilitates this by:<br><br>• Keeping the employee aware of changes in objectives and organizational needs.<br>• Helping the employee understand the impact of change on job requirements, priorities, and the future.<br>• Developing with the employee how any unusual assignments will be completed in terms of importance, scope, timing, approach, facilities, and other factors. |
| 3. The opportunity to participate in planning change and to perform in keeping with ability. | An owner makes this possible by:<br><br>• Seeking and utilizing employee ideas.<br>• Delegating appropriate tasks.<br>• Avoiding excessive supervision and decision making for the employee.<br>• Exercising less control as abilities and confidence improve.<br>• Accepting occasional mistakes as a part of the price of experience. |

4. To receive assistance when needed.

An owner is coaching when he/she:

- Encourages questions and reviews job related problems when help is needed.
- Provides assistance when critical problems arise.
- Makes decisions beyond employee's authority when necessary.

5. To know how well he/she is doing.

An owner communicates how well the employee is doing by:

- Frequently reviewing results in relation to agreed-upon objectives, standards, and changing needs. Gives the employee appropriate feedback.
- Discussing performance in terms of future development every six months.

6. To be recognized and rewarded based on his/her performance.

An owner supports employee performance and growth by:

- Expressing appreciation and providing other recognition at the most appropriate time.
- Commending sustained satisfactory work.
- Recommending or not recommending promotion or reassignment.

7. To work in a climate that encourages self-development.

An owner creates this environment by:

- Establishing a relationship with each employee based on mutual confidence.
- Encouraging and using suggestions and ideas.
- Keeping each employee currently informed of things which affect him/her and the work group.
- Sharing personal philosophies.

As each employee grows through coaching, it is also the responsibility of the coach (manager) to continuously integrate the new skills into effective team performance that supports organizational and personal goals to the maximum possible.

---

*Your Turn*  **Answer the following true/false questions.**

|  | True | False |
|---|---|---|
| 1. Team leaders emphasize each member's involvement and expect that person to take responsibility for his/her contributions. | ☐ | ☐ |
| 2. If you plan to build a strong team and use members' skills to the maximum, there is little need to improve your own skills. | ☐ | ☐ |
| 3. People are more productive when they feel a sense of ownership of the task or of the organization. | ☐ | ☐ |
| 4. When a true team achieves success, so will all of its members. | ☐ | ☐ |
| 5. Selecting qualified people who work well with others at the outset supports team building. | ☐ | ☐ |
| 6. Commitment to task accomplishment is the result when a leader involves team members in planning, goal setting, and problem solving. | ☐ | ☐ |
| 7. Team leaders facilitate training for team members and coach them to apply what has been learned. | ☐ | ☐ |

*Now check your answers with the author's on page 178.*

## Your Turn Answers

1. *True.* Involvement and responsibility are critical to teams.

2. *False.* This is one of the most challenging times ever for leaders.

3. *True.* Ownership builds commitment and responsibility.

4. *True.* Success indicates everyone played their role.

5. *True.* Good people are the foundation for success.

6. *True.* You can't demand it or force it.

7. *True.* Leaders make training useful.

# WHAT IS YOUR ATTITUDE TOWARD COACHING?

Coaching offers one of the best opportunities you have to leave a positive imprint on individual team members, your team as a whole, and the organization. Some owners consider the coaching aspects of their jobs the most rewarding and lasting contributions they can make in the work setting.

What is your attitude toward coaching? Have you given it any constructive thought? Use the scale on the next page to first reflect your attitude toward coaching in the past. Then, after contemplating what you have learned from your personal experience and from reading this book, reflect what you anticipate your attitude toward coaching will be in the future.

| Coaching Applications | Former Attitude Toward Coaching | Future Attitude Toward Coaching |
|---|---|---|
| Coaching is vital to shaping employee performance in the current assignment. | | |
| Coaching enables employees to learn more quickly and reach their level of competence more rapidly. | | |
| Coaching provides a way to help employees achieve their potential as well as tailor that potential to support the skills of other team members. | | |
| Employees accept and adapt more quickly to change when coaching involves them in the process and guides them through. | | |
| Coaching following performance feedback improves the likelihood of positive results. | | |

# CASE STUDY

## Baffled by the Budget

Jack is an excellent department head manager of the manufacturing processes used in his business, but he may have a fatal flaw. He is always over budget and his reasoning about the causes is often weak. This happens even though he prepares the budget himself and personally maintains what appear to be adequate controls. Now his bank has given the company an ultimatum: "Get control of your budget or we will have to cut off additional loans."

Jack's administrative assistant, who has an excellent accounting background, expertise with computers, and some experience with budgets, would like to help. So would his section heads, who believe the budget would be more representative of reality if they had some input. Jack, however, feels it is his responsibility and he has to do it himself.

In the space below, outline what you, as owner, would suggest that Jack do to correct this obviously serious problem.

_____

_____

_____

_____

## Response to Case Study

As owner, you must see to it that Jack releases total control of the budget process in his unit. This will be a diplomatic and coaching test for you. Instead of issuing an order, enlist Jack's help in establishing "team concepts" within his department. Help him envision his new role as team leader.

He should make key staff members responsible for their part of the budget and hold them accountable for results. This means they should participate in the development of the budget and its day-to-day administration. Jack's administrative assistant could be assigned responsibility for pulling the tentative budget together with the help and input of the section heads. When they feel it is complete, they can present it to Jack for review and approval and then follow up to see that everyone stays on track.

# DEVELOPING A PERSONAL ACTION PLAN

Think over the material you have read. Review the self-analysis questionnaires. Rethink the case studies. What have you learned about team building? What did you learn about yourself? How can you apply what you learned? Make a commitment to yourself to become a better team leader and a more effective team builder by designing a personal action plan to help you accomplish this goal.

The following guide may help you clarify your goals and outline actions required to achieve your goals.

1. My current team-leading skills are effective in the following areas:

   _____

   _____

2. I need to improve my team-leading skills in the following areas:

   _____

   _____

3. My goals for improving my team-leading skills are as follows: (Be sure they are specific, attainable and measurable.)

   _____

   _____

4. Following are my action steps, along with a timetable to accomplish each goal.

   _____

   _____

# ASK YOURSELF

► Do I develop and maintain basic management and leadership skills?

► Do I follow good employee selection techniques?

► Do I discuss expectations and participate with employees in setting goals?

► Do I give attention to the training and development needs of team members?

► Do I advocate, support, and nurture team-building activities?

► Do I encourage the involvement of team members in any activity where they could make a contribution?

► Do I provide and receive feedback from the team?

► Do I manage to keep conflict and competition from getting out of control?

► Do I recognize and reward the team and its members?

# ABOUT THE AUTHOR

Robert Maddux is president of Maddux Associates, Consultants in Human Resource Management. He has consulted extensively with large corporations and small businesses over the past twenty years to enable the mutually effective utilization of people in a variety of work environments. He has worked extensively with organizations and people in transition and has been instrumental in facilitating the beginning of many new careers in business organizations and entrepreneurial ventures.

Mr. Maddux has designed and conducted management skills seminars in Canada, Europe and throughout the United States as well as consulting in the production of a number of management training films. He has written many Discussion Leaders' Guides for use in employee development and is the author of several best selling management books including *Team Building: An Exercise in Leadership; Effective Performance Appraisals; Quality Interviewing; Successful Negotiation* and *Delegating for Results.* He is also the co-author of *Job Performance and Chemical Dependency; Guide to Affirmative Action* and *Ethics in Business.*

# THE U.S. CHAMBER OF COMMERCE
# SMALL BUSINESS INSTITUTE

We hope that you found this book beneficial to the success of your operation. For additional materials from the Small Business Institute, refer to the listing below. A free catalog is available upon request from the Small Business Institute, 1200 Hamilton Court, Menlo Park, California 94025. Phone: 800-884-2880

While you are learning, you can also earn a Small Business Institute Certificate of Completion along with valuable continuing education units (CEUs).

| Course materials: | Order Numbers: |
|---|---|
| ***Marketing and Sales*** | |
| Marketing Strategies for Small Businesses | 172-4 |
| Prospecting: The Key to Sales Success | 271-2 |
| Direct Mail Magic | 075-2 |
| Professional Selling | 42-4 |
| Writing and Implementing a Marketing Plan | 083-3 |
| | |
| ***Budget and Finance*** | |
| Financial Basics of Small Business Success | 167-8 |
| Budgeting for a Small Business | 171-6 |
| Extending Credit and Collecting Cash | 168-6 |
| Getting a Business Loan | 164-3 |
| Personal Financial Fitness | 205-4 |
| | |
| ***Legal Issues*** | |
| A Legal Guide for Small Business | 266-6 |
| A Manager's Guide to OSHA | 180-5 |
| Rightful Termination: Avoiding Litigation | 248-8 |
| Sexual Harassment: What You Need to Know | 312-3 |
| The A.D.A.: Hiring, Accommodating and Supervising Employees with Disabilities | 311-5 |
| | |
| ***Human Relations and Communications*** | |
| Human Relations in Small Business | 185-6 |
| Attacking Absenteeism | 42-6 |
| Quality Interviewing | 262-3 |

**U.S. CHAMBER OF COMMERCE**

SMALL
BUSINESS
INSTITUTE™

The publisher of books for the U.S. Chamber of Commerce Small Business Institute is Crisp Publications. Crisp offers over 200 other business and entrepreneurship titles. For more information, call the U.S. Chamber of Commerce Small Business Institute at 800-884-2880.

**CRISP**
PUBLICATIONS